BUSTA RHYME

I SHUFFLE THROUGH MY MIND
TO SEE IF I CAN FIND
THE WORDS I LEFT BEHIND
- GREEN DAY

SOUTH CENTRAL POETS

Edited By Kyra Eyles

First published in Great Britain in 2017 by:

Young Writers
Remus House
Coltsfoot Drive
Peterborough
PE2 9BF
Telephone: 01733 890066
Website: www.youngwriters.co.uk

FOREWORD

Welcome, Reader, to 'Busta Rhyme – South Central Poets'.

For Young Writers' latest poetry competition, we asked our writers to wow us with their words and bust out their bard side!

The result is this collection of fantastic poetic verse that covers a whole host of different topics.

Get ready to be blown away by these passionate poems about love and relationships, school and bullying, equality and human rights, and demanding day-to-day issues that come with living in today's society. This collection has a poem to suit everyone.

Whereas the majority of our writers chose to express themselves with a free verse style, others gave themselves the challenge of other techniques such as acrostics and rhyming couplets.

There was a great response to this competition which is always nice to see, and the standard of entries was excellent, therefore I'd like to say a big thank you and well done to everyone who entered.

Kyra Eyles

CONTENTS

Kennet School, Thatcham

Millside School, Slough

Milton Keynes College, Leadenhall

Sandy Upper School, Sandy

Nicole Tessmer (15)	183
Lara Amy Richards (14)	184
Jamie McEvoy (15)	187
Jakia Jasmin Nessa (15)	188
Eleanor Rose Walker (13)	190
Daniel Walker (15)	191
Caitlin Thomas (15)	192
Ellie Brookes (15)	193
Rio Joseph Samuels (15)	194
Shannon Page Lewinton (15)	195
Jordan James Irvin (15)	196
Caitlin Pearce (14)	197
Ella Symonds (14)	198
Demi Hopkins (15)	199
Jessica Woodward (14)	200
Kye McCann (15)	201
Emily Alice Garlick (15)	202
Daniel Truett (14)	203
Maddy Jakes (14), Daniel & Rosie	204
Riley Jay Lewis Evans (14)	205
Nathan Thomas Costin (15)	206
Emily Kirton (13), Chloe & Lola	207
Shardaya Callari (14)	208

The Milton Keynes Academy, Leadenhall

Ellena Rose Sandford (12)	209
Husnah Iqbal (12)	210
Ittay Socosote (12)	212
Sascha Lilianah Hall (12)	213

The Westgate School, Slough

Julia Galbierczyk (15)	214
Owais Ahmad (17)	217
Breerah Mahmood (15)	218
Tegan Condra (12)	221
Aisha Nadeem (16)	222
Isha Maqsud (14)	224
Zaafira Azhar (14)	226

Oliver Fiore (16)	228
Cassady Byrne (12)	230

THE POEMS

Nature Of Music

Music does not simply appear,
It grows from the heart,
Like a rose from a seedling.
The thorns may sting,
But the orchestra of colour can numb the pain,
The symphony of scents can lull you to sleep,
Like a sweet lullaby.
It is an eternal scar on our covered skin,
It is graffiti on our young impressionable hearts,
It is simply the nature of music.

Julia Normann (12)

Akeley Wood School, Lillingstone Dayrell

Bullies

Tom's fifteen and his life's always been the same
He wakes up, goes to school and deals with his pain
And although he may seem fine
There's only so much someone can hide
So when one day
He's pushed down for being gay
He runs away
He locks himself in the toilets at school
And says he won't come out until he does what he has to do
He takes out the razor he's been hiding for days
And starts to cut his skin away
Blood leaks on from his arm and he cries in pain
He lies on the floor knowing he'll never see the light of day
again

Lilly's fourteen and she hides pills in her bag
She tells her friends that if her parents find out they'll think
she's mad
One day she plans to take her life
Not knowing there's reason to continue the fight
The bullies will taunt her and beat her in school
Nobody says a thing because they're so cool
Their popularity speaks more than their personality
Her peers sit back and watch
Not telling a teacher or parents or someone who can help
Their fear has forced them not to yelp

So when Lilly swallows the pills one by one
Will they feel bad because they're the reason that she's
gone?

When you're hurting someone just for fun
Make sure you think of what's really being done
Or when you're watching someone get beat down on the
ground
And you don't say anything
Are you proud?

Bullying can't go on being ignored, stand up for those being
hurt and who fought.

Louanna Gemmell (14)
Cardinal Newman Catholic School - A Specialist Science College, Luton

All Lives Matter!

Whether you are black, white, Asian or even mixed race, all
of our lives matter!
Let's forget about the past
Put our differences behind us at last
Black people are seen as thieves and gang members
The Feds see them on the streets in hoodies and think
they're up to something bad
But for all you know, they are just buying medicine for their
sick mum
They may be on their way to church or even volunteering to
help the needy
But these other races don't see that or know that
Asians are seen as terrorists or Isis members
Only here to bomb places and take lives away whilst
shouting, 'Praise God' (God be the glory)
The're seen as only here to take people's lives away
Some see Asians and just run away
But for all you know they were on their way to buy their sick
sister some medicine
Or going to the mosque or getting away from people
judging them
But all these other races don't know that or see that
White people are seen to be all the same
Too proud, too vain and always hate
Don't like different people or different cultures
Go out to make fun of people's differences
But for all you know they love different people and different
cultures

But all these other races don't know that or see that
So let's not judge each other and let's come together as one
and be one big family
Let's put our differences aside
It only matters about what's inside.

Annalisa Owusu (13)

Cardinal Newman Catholic School - A Specialist Science College, Luton

Equality

People are constantly blinded by hate
But why do humans always discriminate?
We're all the same, a heart, a face
So what if some of us are a different race?

So what if we're gay? Or bi? Or queer?
We all have a heart, a brain and ears
So what is they're trans? Or fluid? Or straight?
It's not your life, so why do you hate?

Society's expectations, why are they so high?
Raised by social media, nothing but a lie?
Pictures are edited, photos are cropped
Everybody wake up! It has to stop!

'Black lives matter', of course they do!
People didn't fight slavery to be stopped by you
'Dumbo blondes' and 'smart Asians' are stereotypes
It's time to stop the system, time to rewrite!

Slaves, suffragettes, prisoners of war
Why are we still fighting? Why is there more?
We don't choose who we are, that's how it is!
Gay people and black people have never been born in a bin

You have the nerve to say we're all the same?
Yeah we are, but we're different in our own way
We're the same species, a family, a team
How do you have more rights than me?

Ciara McAree (13)
Cardinal Newman Catholic School - A Specialist Science College, Luton

All People Are Equal

It happens every day
They say we are all equal but
They don't practise what they preach
Women fought for equal rights
People say they got it
Are pay gaps and stereotypes and sexism equality?
If this is equality then the fight is still ongoing
Women are not objects or robots or servants for men
They are individuals
Men aren't the only happiness in a woman's life
They can live it without them
Growing up, girls are made to dream of house keeping and
husbands and children
Boys are allowed to dream of anything
It's forced down our throats
Boys are messy, girls are clean
Girls live at home, boys can dream
It's time to break the line
And it's not just with girls and boys
A white man or black man are the same
But are different in their own way
Names are not the same
Different in their own way, as what's in a name?
Equality is more than just a word
And if that's the one thing you learn from this then,
Case closed.

Poppy Smith (13)

Cardinal Newman Catholic School - A Specialist Science College, Luton

Stereotyping

Some may think that they're the better race
Cos they feel they have better taste
Or that they're the superior gender
And that the opposite sex is way too tender

Maybe they think that a particular skin type only commits
crime
And that they should serve extra time
Or possibly that not being average height or weight
May always lead to a bad fate

Another thing, people may judge materialistic things
The more money you have, you're practically a king
Perhaps they think a particular religion is a complete
shambles
And believers of that religion are all scandals

But what people may forget to see
We're all quite similar, take time to look; you'll agree
An X-ray doesn't pick up any of these stereotypes
But the unique things, a bit like the uniqueness, like a
zebra's stripes

So ignore the bad things people may say
That may lead you entirely astray
And the rumours that they have told
Be the better person, be brave, be bold

Because you are you
Don't change for anyone, especially to fit in a crew.

Janet Mbaike (14)

Cardinal Newman Catholic School - A Specialist Science College, Luton

Anxiety

Dear Anxiety
Why do you feel there's benefit
For making me feel irrelevant, defect
Just for the hell of it to make me feel like
I just can't do or be anything, any of it okay
Call me a hypocrite
For me making everyone else feel like it
But there is no other
Way of living for me because it just smothers
Any idea of getting out

We could be having a conversation but sorry
I'll have a lack of concentration
Because my brain's too focused on nervousness to follow
any legislation
No grammar, no punctuation
My depth of thought has no limitation
No boundary of the imagination
Not able to process any information
Because I'm scared if you

I go to school to learn
Sitting restless, fidgeting because my shin burns
Stomach churns
Heart yearns

Because I'm not at home, can't wait to return
To where I finally feel safer from anxiety
Although I never really am.

Caoimhe Burke

Cardinal Newman Catholic School - A Specialist Science College, Luton

Our World

Justice is what people need, picking the tobacco that we don't need
What is beauty placed in the head?
The beauty within is what matters instead
Past people before us slaving for rights
Now we live freely, is that right?

Society changes so we do
Racist remarks, that's what we do?
The Lord made us to live in harmony
Now all we do is fight dramatically
Wars that bad people have started for things like oil and gold
So it can be divided

This imagine in our head that these things are good
Tap into your brain, is this how it started?

Out on a ship, rows and rows to be sold again
Look at this; no!
Education is what's needed to make this world right
Billions and billions just for a night
People don't bother to help but put it on TV
We are gonna help the people, they'll be free
What has our world come to today?
All we need to do is just pray.

Ambe Abemnwi Fru Ndefru (12)
Cardinal Newman Catholic School - A Specialist Science College, Luton

Poverty

Poverty, that's all I'm going to say, poverty
Buying shoes we don't need, jewellery, diamonds, gold, we waste money
Instead of money we buy things we don't need, withdrawing money from the cash machine
Buying doughnuts and slushies
We waste water on a daily basis, not liking food, not thinking about other countries
Hungry humans everywhere, India, Africa, Saudi Arabia
People thinking we should stay from their area
Poverty, poverty, poverty
People buying cars, not thinking about global warming
The money for cars, we could have bought clothing
Look at our society, we're wealthy
Look at theirs, they are in poverty
We need to help Kenya, Namibia and Tasmania
No food, no water, no paper
Diseases, illness, dying from severe bleeding
We need to help our society, to stop poverty
Look at all these families
Children with nothing to eat
Poverty.

Clyde Anthony Labe Jison (13)
Cardinal Newman Catholic School - A Specialist Science College, Luton

People In Society

Society
You see white
You see black
You see mixed
You see brown

When you see a Muslim
All you think is terrorist
When you see a black person
All you think is gangs
When you see a white person
You stop and think
What are they, they ruled, now we're equal?

Racism still exists today
But it hides in the shadows
You see a white man steal
You see a black man steal
You should have the same reaction
But you don't

You see a gay person
You stay away
You see a homeless person
You stay away
You see a disabled person
You stay away

But stop and think
What if you were like this
What if you were gay or homeless
Or disabled? Would people look at you the same way you
looked at them?

Morgan Ahern (15)

Cardinal Newman Catholic School - A Specialist Science College, Luton

Ode To Minecraft

A couple of years ago, around 2009
Some people made a game where you could craft and mine
Mojang was their name and they released it to the nations
Within a year or two, it became a sensation

Break and place blocks, that was the simple spark
Then came the zombies, and a wild wolf's bark
Creepers, spiders, all of them would come out at night
So you had to find shelter, or get ready to fight

It got bigger and bigger, oh you bet
Some players posted, 'Let's play on the net'
Sparklex, Bajan, they're just two
Dan, Sky and Stampy, a famous few

So every day, I boot up my PlayStation
And play the game that touched several nations
I go to my worlds, made entirely of blocks
Where the only limit is my imagination.

Paul Masterson (13)
Cardinal Newman Catholic School - A Specialist Science College, Luton

Her Identity

She looks in the mirror, wondering who she is
She looks at her figure, wondering if she's pretty enough
She's pretty enough
The next day
School
It starts with name calling and ends with a punch in the stomach
She's scared
She hurts all over
She slowly walks to her next lesson
Frightened at lunch
She sits in the toilet
Wondering when it will end

A few weeks later
She sees a curvy model in the magazine
She smiles
She runs downstairs to her mum
She explains everything
Her mum cuddles her

The next week
She goes to school with nothing to worry about
At lunch she's happy
She sits with her friends
She goes to her next lesson, skipping.

Danielle Susan Quille (12)
Cardinal Newman Catholic School - A Specialist Science College, Luton

My Poem

Oh, it's you, the one who threw rubbish on the floor
Why don't you go to the bin any more?
Other countries have to store their trash on the floor
Causing infection to pass through the place
Do you even care any more?

I hear an old factory got smashed down
Empty space is there today
Think of the things we can build today
People are begging to live in a house today
Help create a place for them to stay

Would you ever give up your car today
To prevent the Antarctic from melting again?
Some people are dehydrated today because the water is
dirty and infected
Cafod and Fairtrade are helping poor people today
And that's my poem, please read this and care.

Emmanuel Owusu Acheampong (12)
Cardinal Newman Catholic School - A Specialist Science College, Luton

Education

People take education for granted, swearing, shouting in class, it's pointless
Your teachers try to help you to succeed but it doesn't work, you don't care, don't care
You start to panic, writing test is coming up, you never revised
If you did and tried your best well then so be it
Be confident, smart, wise, you'll be able to strive for your goal
And maybe, just maybe, you'll succeed
You control your future, think about it now and just hope, and you have teachers, family and friends there for you
Make those who love you proud and they can see you try
They'll help you
Just try, try, try your best and then you'll realise you have a hidden talent to help you along the way.

Caoimhin Travers (13)

Cardinal Newman Catholic School - A Specialist Science College, Luton

Labels

Society gave us labels
They tie us down
Create all the racism
They thought it would be a good idea
But all it did was tear us apart
Destroying our relationships
Creating an ongoing war

If we look at two babies
Playing together
We see no racism
Why?

Society teaches us to be racist
White to black
Christian to Muslim
Trump to everyone

Only together will we stop this
And like a tree if we want to end it
We don't stand by the branches
But we stand by the root
And by cutting the root
We will end this all
And get rid of all these labels
To be one community again
One loving label called
Humankind.

Gabriel Serra (14)
Cardinal Newman Catholic School - A Specialist Science College, Luton

Global Warming/Politics

As we open up the carbon gates
And make the world inflate
To decide on the future kids' lives
Then let all the politicians be wise
To make all decisions as if we have no say
Until the day I pass away
But until this day comes I want my kids to have the way
Of the grand rules that lay
And not to let them walk through the doorway without
setting the public display
With a thorough essay and not let them outweigh my kids to
go up the runway

As we open up the carbon gates
And make the world inflate
To decide on the future kids' lives
Then let all the politicians be wise
To make all decisions as if we have to say
Until the day I pass away.

Joshua Darmanin (15)
Cardinal Newman Catholic School - A Specialist Science College, Luton

The Invisible

Invisible is who I am
Blinded by hatred as I walk out
I never knew a single pout
Or shout
Or not being very loud
Would affect me by who I am
Walking alone, snakes behind me
Slithering up so they can down me
I avoid their traps so they won't see
Who I really am as me
Sitting down, people staring
If only they knew how much I was tearing
Looking away, tears were streaming
Making fun of me because of dreaming
No one knows
No one cares
People ignoring my desperate stares
Lowering down
With a frown
If only they knew how it felt like to be me
Invisible forever, it may seem.

Huda Israr (14)

Cardinal Newman Catholic School - A Specialist Science College, Luton

Past Tense

He was just fourteen years old
He wore glasses and had spots on his face
He had no friends
He wasn't cool like all the other kids
His shoes were worn and ripped due to his parents' poor wealth
He couldn't concentrate in class, pens and all sorts would be thrown at him
His school bag was old and torn
All the other kids would laugh and snigger at his appearance
Occasionally he would get a nudge in the back
Teachers wouldn't care
Parents wouldn't care
His mum hated him
He was skinny, like a twig
He hated life so much
So much he couldn't take it.

Alex Brinklow (13)
Cardinal Newman Catholic School - A Specialist Science College, Luton

Untitled

As you circle the world round and round you hear the sound
of globalisation
People fight for equality and rights that will give them
freedom of speech and choice
Europa divided into many of the vast amounts of ideological
views
Liberal and nationalist against one another
One insulted by the other, called a racist or a divider of their
culture
One gives all and the other for their own
One spreading the false message of globalism with the
other, a so-called fascist
A red cross on their backs awaiting for the right moment
The sound fades as you venture into the quiet abyss of
space.

Jakub Mariusz Kaczmarek (14)
Cardinal Newman Catholic School - A Specialist Science College, Luton

School

So much pressure put on me
Why won't everybody leave me be?
Why am I learning what's pi times ten
Why not just teach me life skills instead?
I'd be happier laying in my bed
Waking up to be punished for my shoes
No reds, no blues, it's black you should choose
Being asked questions, when I have no clues
There's so much on my mind, I don't want to lose
But lose I do, as tests are not my thing
But I hope my future is filled with bling
Money, wealth, riches, cha-ching
But to get all that I'll need to win.

Alex Lamontagne-Charles (15)

Cardinal Newman Catholic School - A Specialist Science College, Luton

Angels

Angels, angels, angels
Soaring and flying across the sky
Why me? Why'd you take him
Time so timeless, limits so limitless
We have the world, it has us
Dine with me, sweet angel
Die with us in this savage world
Angels, angels, angels
Why'd you take him?
Why so far, sorrow into the sky
Never to be seen or heard again
Distant memories, latch on them before it's late
Angels grasping onto this timeless life
Never to be seen or heard of
Goodbye sweet angel
Meet you in sinister heaven.

Damilola Akinjise-Ferdinand (15)

Cardinal Newman Catholic School - A Specialist Science College, Luton

Sonnet WW2

Oh no, again the war has started
Let's hope not as many people died
They will shoot with a machine gun
So that we have more planes shooting through the sky
I said goodbye to my gran
My gran was really sad
Then something went *bang!*
Oh isn't the war so bad?
A place malfunctioned with a leak
As the plane had a malfunction
It fell from the sky at its peak
The explosion was a massive eruption
This is based on World War 2
When the next war is, I haven't a clue.

Daniel James Fielder (14)

Cardinal Newman Catholic School - A Specialist Science College, Luton

They Will Always Forget

Whenever I walk down the street with my brother
All of the haters shout out at my mother
They scowl at him with no bother

I throw dirty looks back at them
To show them how it feels
They kill their teeth
But we stomp our heels

They call him Dumbo and it feels like
A dagger in our hearts
We throw it back
It breaks them apart

They will forget but we
Will always remember

They will forget but we will always remember.

Hannah Pearce (12) & Amy Kasembe (12)
Cardinal Newman Catholic School - A Specialist Science College, Luton

Images

Yellow, pink and blue, I actually have no clue
In each image there's a colour
Whatever the colour: green, white, black or grey
There is a colour for you

Huge, small, average, you know that is true
Whatever it is, it's a masterpiece for someone, even you
Some think *what is that?* Others think *fabulous* or even
spontaneous
In the end an image is an image no matter what
Some good, some bad, everything is about your opinion.

Leonardo Baptista (13)

Cardinal Newman Catholic School - A Specialist Science College, Luton

Education Poem

Be grateful for the education you have
Be thankful for the creation of the world
For your mum and dad
Children as young as five are acting immature
Other children are copying instead of reading books
and being mature
Education is an adventure to explore new things, to have a
good future
Some have no education, let's work hard and study so you
can prepare for your graduation
Then you can teach others to do the same.

Mary Foresythe (13)
Cardinal Newman Catholic School - A Specialist Science College, Luton

War

It loves to create chaos
It loves to create fear inside us
It is made of negativity and panic
It feeds from this
Although the war has ended
And there is peace between us
It lingers waiting to thrive and grow
Planning its next attack on humans
Corrupting people is what it does
Feeding their minds with false theories
Stealing our lives away from us.

Juliann Mbaje (14)

Cardinal Newman Catholic School - A Specialist Science College, Luton

Differences

We are all people
But some
Put labels on us
She may be white, she may be mixed race
But we're all a part of the human race
She might be geeky, she might be popular
But they're just looks...

Who cares about skin tones?
Who cares about hair?
Who cares about being popular?
They're all just labels.

Luizela Aaliyah Carvaho (12) & Kaitlyn Doherty
Cardinal Newman Catholic School - A Specialist Science College, Luton

The World Around Us

Walls are falling
EU crumbling
Scotland arguing
Britain dying

Trump commanding
Mexicans are paying
Labour is losing
Kim Jong-Un planning
Nuke tests happening

Royal weddings are happening
Inventions are helping
New lives are born
Welcome to our world.

Gabriel Butterfield (12) & Mateusz

Cardinal Newman Catholic School - A Specialist Science College, Luton

Who Are We?

Do we know who we are?
Some people held to a higher bar
Dreaming of who we could be
Thinking about what people see

Trying to be a different me
Everyone else got so much glee
We are very different from each other
No one else even bothers.

Jaweria Zakiya Saleem (14)
Cardinal Newman Catholic School - A Specialist Science College, Luton

Education

We take it for granted
Our future is nothing without it
We spend most of our childhood there
But time goes by fast
Bang, suddenly you get a job
Have a family
Get a career
It all went by so fast.

Maisie Yanguas Street

Cardinal Newman Catholic School - A Specialist Science College, Luton

We Were Born To Be Real, Not To Be Perfect

A girl was born
With her first clothes worn
Crying and crying
In her motherland

Close your eyes
Open your eyes
She is talking
Clap your hands
She is walking
Look behind you
She is going
Going to school
Go to bed
Sleep
Wake up
She is writing

Give her your hands
Full of glitter
And sprinkle her life
Trick her!
Get her laughing
And having nice moments
She can remember

Give her
A white heart
A kind heart
A heart doesn't know
How to be sad
Give her two brothers
And make her jealous
Last request please!
Give her a family with
Warmth and kindness
That she can feel
Let her survive
And drive
With her life
For eight years

Watching TV
Going to school
Having fun
Dreaming to travel
All around the world
And that is
Her dream world!

Time to stop
Her life was
Sprinkled by
Special glitter

Travelling all around the world
Without saying any word
With her hair curled
Dancing like a bird

She didn't know
If she had to be
Happy or
Crazy
Sad or
Mad
And before all that
Running like a cat
Off from her land

Now the girl who was born
Is thirteen
Wearing jeans
The girl who was crying
In her motherland
Now she is dying
For her land
And dreams of seeing
Her motherland
The girl who started to talk
Now she is shouting
She wants her nice
Memories back

The girl who started to write
Now she is writing poems
For her land
The girl who started to walk
Now she is
Running
Searching
And hoping
To find a way to get
Her land back
The girl who had
A kind, open heart
Now her heart is closing from
Other's rudeness
The girl who had her family beside
Now everyone is left
From the east to the west

No one
Can hear her
No one
Can feel her
No one
Can see her
She is sad
Not glad
Not mad

All she can hear
Is bombs
All she can see
Is people dying
And escaping from her land
Her land is disappearing
Buildings are crashing and falling down
On the ground
And she
She is here
With her smile on her lips
Surviving
Living
And leaving.

Lara Al-Hindi (13)
Gosford Hill School, Kidlington

Football

What I love about football is that the ball floats up into the sky as an eagle is scavenging for prey,
What I hate about fouls is the moment of truth and when you're getting cards for just a single move,
What I love about football is the techniques and plays though the match, giving you a sensation that you never felt,
What I hate about players is the effort that they give in the match when they could be much better,
What I love about the game is the speed of the game itself,
What I hate about the manager is that there are more and more things to do when we always improve,
What I love about the referee is that he gives us big opportunities and big chances and a feeling of clear hope,
What I hate about the fans is that they cheer too much and at the end they always make a mess,
What I love about football is that a lot of languages and nationalities are spoken around us, giving you a warm sensation,
What I hate about football is that you always have to move teams to the worst one,
What I love about football is the chemistry, no matter what happens you still work together,
What I hate about the rain is that when you give your whole power it slowly and simply falls as a forgotten memory.

Leo Havalescu (14)
Gosford Hill School, Kidlington

Power

Here it is
Power
Power is something we cannot see
Everyone cherishes but some disagree
With what power can create
And how it leaves people free

And they see the light

They saw the light and he saw the dream
He had a dream, I had a dream

He saw the dream and made white black, black white
Now they see the light
But the light is unclean
They saw the light, they saw the dream, they saw the power, and they felt the power
Now they have the power and the power is gone, it is
Money it's
Passion it's
Democracy
And the people have power

Now the people have power and the power has dreams
And the dreams are of money and power and schemes
And they have the power

And how it seems they have something to prove
They want problems and answers
They have nothing to lose!

So now they have nothing
They see the light fall far away
They are reaching, they reach
But they all reach in vain!

But oh!
What is this?
It claws to the surface
A smile on its face
And greed is its name

And that greed is dark
And the light is long lost
Alas! Alas!
The world is astray
Where is the beauty?

The beauty is lost, in place of the light and the dream there
is rot
Some people are lost, astray
Some people did reach but they all reached in vain!

One stayed long
And wisdom prevailed
And they had a dream
And made white black, black white

That one person believes we all should be free
Out of the belief grew freedom, conspiracy
One disagrees and believes in rights
This bore equality; along with it fright!
Of the wilting green

They watched the flower wilt, and one broke away
They believed they too had something to say
And this little burst of outrage
Grew the lies and schemes of our age
And this little flower blossomed
Into
Grief which bore sadness
Which bore happiness, kindness
Which bore jealousy, honesty
Which bore truths and then policies
Which bore power, incentives
Democracy

And now one person wants freedom, another wants rights
and another wishes the world could be green
Are you confused? Well so are we
Where do they go from here?

Beth Fransham (12)
Gosford Hill School, Kidlington

Love And Hate

What I love about sloths is that they are really slow and lazy
What I hate about tigers is that they are really crazy
What I love about friendship is that people are always there for you
What I hate about siblings is that they scare you and say boo
What I love about my dad is that he is always proud of me
What I love about football is seeing all the different nationalities
What I hate about Optic is that they think they are better than Faze
What I love about Tiago is that we made a sniping clan called Haze
What I love about sniping on Call of Duty is that it inspired me to join Faze Clan
What I hate about my phone is that it dies on 100% when I'm playing Clash of Clans
What I hate love about the Flash is it is a popular TV show
What I hate about weddings is that you have to wear a bow or tie
What I hate about life is seeing people die
What I love about my brother is that he looks very smart in a shirt and tie
What I hate about the new smart car is that it looks like a cube
What I hate about maths is that we are learning about cuboids
What I love about my family is that they are the most loving things in the world.

Kyle Uren-Palmer (13)
Gosford Hill School, Kidlington

This Is Me I Am Describing To You

A girl with blue eyes
A girl with blonde hair
This is me I am describing to you

With her hair as bright as sand
And her eyes like the sea
This is me I am describing to you

The love of singing
The love of drawing
This is me I am describing to you

Her parents apart
With two houses to live in
This is me I am describing to you

The hair getting darker
Whilst the girl gets older
This is me I am describing to you

Laughter and happiness
With her friends and family
This is me I am describing to you

When she supports one team
But others support another
This is me I am describing to you

Favourite artists
Ed, Adele and 1D
This is me I am describing to you

Creativity and visiting family
Baking and motorbikes
This is me I am describing to you

The jealousy of two cousins
Then of a brother
This is me I am describing to you

With school being important to her
Like a leaf to a tree
This is me I am describing to you

Lessons she likes
Such as maths, English and maybe science
This is me I am describing to you

Family and friends
To her is her life
This is me I am describing to you

Spending time with her pets
Involving cuddles and playing games
This is me I am describing to you

Being outside
And enjoying the sun
This is me I am describing to you

With small things making her laugh
And many people confused
This is me I am describing to you

Colour and brightness
And happiness all day
This is me I am describing to you

Family walks to the river
Where her dog swims and plays
This is me I am describing to you

Friends calling her friendly
And someone who makes them smile
This is me I am describing to you

With her being crazy
But positive and happy too
This is me I am describing to you

The love of adventure
And the love of the outdoors
This is me I am describing to you

This is me, who I am
Not who you want to be
And this is the end of me describing myself to you!

Lyndsay Louise Marsh (13)
Gosford Hill School, Kidlington

Terrorists

They don't understand
Just killing innocent people, just to prove their power
The families of the people's lives that have been taken
All the news stories and headlines in newspapers
But they are punished by death
Everyone is so worried about if it will happen to them
Terrorists are just the worst thing to happen to this world

9/11 is just one of their sickening attacks
I can't imagine what it was like on that plane
Some people going back home from their holidays
Not knowing that a few minutes after take-off they would
crash

But the attacks I most worry about is the ones here
Like the attack in London and the one in Manchester
I'm worried about them the most because they are affecting
families here and not just where they live

So I say to the terrorists, stop, think about all the
destruction
All the damage and most importantly, think about the
families

But they probably will never stop their evil ways
So we can just hope that they will realise the damage they
caused to all the people affected by their pointless attacks.

David Butler (13)
Gosford Hill School, Kidlington

Your Heart Will Always Be Mine

When I lay there beside you
Could you feel me there?
My arms wrapped around you
And I was stroking your hair

I was talking about our good times
For me these were every single day
I want you to feel love and comfort
And happy in some way

I watched your every breath
And prayed each one wasn't your last
The time we got to share together
Went by too quick... too fast

I wanted you to wake up
Please Nan... open your eyes
Tell me this is a nightmare
And not our goodbyes

As your last breath grew closer
We lay there peacefully together
My heart continually breaking
Because I wanted you forever

Your final breath of air
I didn't want to believe it
This is so cruel and not fair
I held your beautiful face

And prayed you'd breathe again
I wasn't ready for you to go
I couldn't admit that this was the end
But then I realised that you are now in peace

And not suffering any more
You were beginning the life of an angel
And your body will no longer be sore
I held you close and squeezed you tight

And tried to say goodbye
I've lost my nan and my number one best friend
All my heart could do is cry
I slowly get up

I wanted so much to stay
I leaned over and gave you one more kiss
It was so hard to walk away
Nan, you are my world

And I miss you so very much
I wish I could feel your lovable cuddles
And your sense of humour and gentle touch
But for now I have to wait
Until we meet again

You will always be in my heart
And thoughts
My dear nan and best friend
Always and forever

Our hearts will always touch
Always and forever
Your granddaughter loves you so much.

Calliesha Harris (13)
Gosford Hill School, Kidlington

One Day

The wind blows left and right
A storm is coming, it's in sight
A dark cloud is reigning and sadness lingers
The feeling rises from her toes to her fingers
There's a lump on her throat and her stomach is churning
Her palms are sweating, her heart is burning
Her world stops, the words blur out
All she wants to do is scream and shout
For this girl has seen the cruel world in all its reality
The war, the bombs, the pure humanity
This girl never wished to be a princess or Power Ranger
All she's ever wanted is to escape from the danger
This international fight, we're in it together
If we don't start now it will go on forever
That girl's just a girl, so innocent and kind
But when she sees the horrid world, she'll want to leave it behind
If you're reading this poem, do something for me
But ignore the war torn countries and the poverty
The hunger is around us and soon you'll see
But know this, tomorrow it could be you or me
I know I'm just a girl and I don't have much say
But I hope you'll help me clear up that storm one day.

Mia Corness (13)
Gosford Hill School, Kidlington

The Journey Called Life

I'm sat down wondering what to write
My passion? My hobbies? My future job?
No idea how this poem will turn out
The unknown isn't scary

Trying to figure the future is a maths test
There are puzzles and problems and lots of preparation
It could result in good or bad
Needs hard work and determination

You may be thinking, what does this have to do with life?
I see your point, you have to wait

Life is unknown
Your life is unknown
Everybody's life is unknown
This poem is unknown
Impossible to predict but possible to prepare for
The future of your life comes with excitement

Not knowing is okay
In fact, it's better than okay, it's great!
If you know exactly what will happen at every moment
Like the next note Beethoven will play in his new piece
Your life will be just as boring as watching a snail move 100
metres
Yes! That boring

Life is a road
A road with many different turns
Many different stops
Many different routes coming off
There are so many opportunities and that is what makes it
exciting
Worth preparing for and worth living
There isn't only an end and a beginning!

I am not the one for advice
Maybe not the one for poems
But all I say is
Prepare, work hard
And take the opportunities going

Bang! Like this you could be offered a trip to...
Australia
Italy
Timbuktu
Spain
France
Or even the moon!

Nobody knows what life has in store
Treat it like a birthday with many surprises
I'm sure you don't want everything to be a bore!

I wanted this poem to move with a little twist
Like the journey called life.

Katy Mills (13)
Gosford Hill School, Kidlington

Five

Stage one:
The first stage is most commonly known as denial
But you deny that, like someone denying illness while
coughing up bile
You don't believe what you see or hear
But that's the point
You're not here
There are people all around you, grieving, just like you
But it's different, for your loss is yourself

Stage two:
The second stage is most commonly known as anger
The pain opens its flood gates
And lowers its anchor
It was a tidal wave, and you weren't prepared
Broken, so broken, broken beyond repair
But the anger subsides
Until there's only resentment towards yourself

Stage three:
The third stage is most commonly known as bargaining
Foolishly, you waste your mind bartering with empty space
Wishing to postpone, another time, another place
It's all useless! You chose to meet
The face of death

But as you take your last breath
And look at what's left
You beg and plead
Get down on your knees
Only to find you did this is yourself

Stage four:
The fourth stage is most commonly known as depression
Your mentality is in turmoil, an everlasting concussion
You're drowning, you're dying
You can't stop crying
The weight is pushing harder, harder
Your heart is failing
Your face is paling
And you think you did this to yourself

Stage five:
The fifth stage is most commonly known as acceptance
The weight is a small pebble now
But always there
The people you knew, they're there, they cared
You're gone now, never to return
The five stages, it's their turn
It's horrifying how easy it is to lose yourself.

Chloe Kerr (13)
Gosford Hill School, Kidlington

Losing A Love

When you first lose someone
I'll be there
And when you find someone new
I'll pretend not to care

Time's gone by
And something's not right
You don't seem OK
That gives me a fight

I know you're slipping away
It's only a matter of days
Soon there'll be nothing
You'll disappear in a haze

Close your eyes
It's alright, my dear
I know you're in pain
I'll always be here

I tell you we'll meet again
This time in the stars
We'll be free
This world'll be ours

As you take your last breaths
You say my name
You're not strong any more
I've seen your weak frame

A tear runs down my cheek
You say I'll be fine
But I'm not too sure
You say that I'll shine

You're leaving this Earth
You're gasping for air
You're in pain
And that's just not fair

Goodbye, my dear
I'll see you soon
I kiss you goodbye
You're off to the moon

Years have gone by
And I only want you
Everything's so dim
But the sky's so blue!

Finally, it's my turn
I'll see you soon
Not that long now
I'm off to the moon!

So we meet again
Happy as can be
No more pain
And as free as can be

We're together my dear
I knew we would be
Peaceful and free
No more rough seas

We walk along the clouds
Our hands intertwined
The sun shines brightly
We're perfectly aligned!

Demi Nairn (13)
Gosford Hill School, Kidlington

Dark Screens

With the push of a button, on it goes
Tapping the screen it goes to show
We're being enslaved by technology
Day after day
Night after night
Technology isn't good
In fact, it's generally misunderstood

People out there are driven into sadness and depression
Like it's the cold-hearted bullies' mission
Tap, tap, tap and the damage is done with all the offensive
stuff
Until the victim decides enough is enough
Sometimes they take their own life
All because of technology
Technology rules our life

All kids do is stare down at their screens
They just blank out the magnificent scenes
Even when they cross the road
Their eyes glued to the screen like they're stuck in a mode
Sometimes they don't look up in time
And as the pool of cold blood forms, right there is a crime
How can people misunderstand
The severe damage people can cause with just their hand?
Because of this people lose their lives
How technology has destroyed many people's lives...

Camron Christopher (13)
Gosford Hill School, Kidlington

Basketball

Basketball
It's not a sport, it's a lifestyle
No one understands it
What it means to play it
For the money
The fame
But mainly for the love of the game
Basketball, it's not a sport
It's a lifestyle

As I dribble down the court
I hear the whistle blow
The ref yells out two shots
And sends me for a free throw
I make my first shot, it goes down with a swish
But for my second shot I could only wish
I really want to make it
Go ahead and save the game
But instead I airballed and felt really lame
Coach called a time out and said, 'I want the ball.'
Steal it on the throw in and we will win it all
The centre throws the ball in and our player jumps in front
He throws his little hands up and the ball goes *bump*
It's in the air now and it is right where I can see
So I jump as high as I can and it lands right on me
I dribble to the three point line, stopped and popped a shot
But next thing that I knew it bounced right out

The teams scrambled for a rebound, we're still trailing them
by three
But out of nowhere our team grabs the ball and throws it
back out to me
When I shoot the ball I shoot like a waterfall
I try to take the three again and this time it's a wish
Swish, swoosh are the sounds it makes when I bang the
basketball into the hoop
I never could have done it without our team's dish
My coach said I saved the game with my amazing shot
He jumped up and down and celebrated quite a lot
The opposition asked me how I did it
I said all you need to do is work hard, have passion and
determination.

Aman Kalyan (13)
Gosford Hill School, Kidlington

Dad!

The bright colours have turned dark
You couldn't cope any longer
So we drifted apart
I was only young, I didn't understand

I hate it when everyone talks about the way you were
I thought you had changed but the truth is
You never did and I don't think you ever will

Memories of you haunt me
The good and the bad
The truth is I want to forget all about you
All of the pain and stress you have put my family through
I just wonder how you could actually do that to the
Even though they were always there for you
I don't know why
You've chosen your chances for the last time
It's not that easy to forget about you
We used to be closer
But it's your fault that me and the person who I feel I should
be the closest to
Feels like the person is furthest away from

I forgot all about you for a while
When I was younger
But the truth is it was your fault, you couldn't cope so you
left

You have never really felt like my dad
You were hardly there
Every time you want me to see you
There's always a way to let me down
So many excuses, so many lies

I hate the way you are
But I know you can't change
And it's not your fault, but it makes everyone want to move
away from you

In the end you will be all alone
Then you will do what you do best
Lie, make up excuses to make people sorry for you
And then it will repeat all over again
Unless you change for the better

But there is still some love
Somewhere deep down inside.

Eden Cullen
Gosford Hill School, Kidlington

Shell Shock

A silence at night
A strong silence with fright
With the mind as sharp as a razor
Hearing the bangs, bangs and bangs,
In pain waiting for it to end
It's insane fighting... The sighting of it brings fear slowly
trickling down my spine,
Bringing chills with the slightest touch,
This is a war, a war to end all wars.
Bang, bang
I'm on the floor, the taste of the dust slowly demolishing my
body,
I'm hoping for a door, a door to run, a door to survive,
Wordlessly I cry, waiting for my escape in the trenches,
The feeling of the dirt clawing at me makes me get up... But
I can't move *Bang, bang*
Release me... release me from this pain.
I try hard but end up turning insane,
The screams echo through my head,
The screams of innocent people dying... it was said that,
This is the best thing for all,
Especially me,
Me! I regret the choice, It's the worst I've ever made.
This lie This broken tie of faith and trust, tarnished.
It's gone... It's all gone!
Slowly grasping for mercy, slowly grasping for freedom.

The bittersweet feeling of death awaits.
Dreadful death daring.
Even my enemies' friends are my enemies.
Bang, bang.
Some of the men muttering and gazing upon others and me.
In an awe-struck attitude... it was extremely clear he'd gone
firing and cursing.
Without mercy he kills my friends.
Now I gaze upon him as a war devil.
Bang, bang.
I open death into my arms.

Joseph Sarbatta (13)
Gosford Hill School, Kidlington

Playdream

Childhood was a whirlpool of imagination
Me and my mates fighting Lego creations
Playing with sticks pretending we were wielding swords
Mowing down waves of zombie hordes
Running through the park holding up our hands
Pretending they're guns and yelling, 'Bang!'

But now we've grown up, stressing about exams
Looked down upon if we hold up our hands
Pretending they're guns and yelling, 'Bang!'
We spend our break times stood having a talk
Or when the weather is hot, playing football
But all of this, it's not the same
As when we were little, playing our games

Without the freedom of our imaginations
We end up resorting to fantasy simulations
Video games are how we have fun
Apart from the occasional mess around in the sun
Our avatar's swords dance through the hordes
Slaying orcs by the dozen and mages with wards
Building civilisations with godly power
Racing each other at 200 miles an hour
Mining and crafting
Building some daft things
Overthrowing the mighty king

All of these things we do together
And as always with friends, it's so much better
The problem is you don't see them face-to-face
Over Xbox Live when you're having a race
Like you would if you were messing around in the sun
Riding your bikes and having fun
So it's really sad when you call their phones
And the answer is, 'Please leave a message after the tone.'

Daniel Andrew (13)
Gosford Hill School, Kidlington

But Do We Care?

We are not all good
Polluting air without a care
From factories to vehicles
Littering the streets, towns and nature reserves
This is not what they deserve
Poaching animals for hide and fur
Oh why does this occur?

African families struggling and bare:
No food, no water, but do we care?
As long as we have a signal on our mobile phones
It is then we hear no more groans!

Global warming is another problem
Using up energy, electricity and gas
Would felicity resolve the shortage?
Please note with care
Wasting unrenewable resources
Will leave us in poverty

We are not all bad
Recycled waste is placed in bins
This is where it all begins
Rehoming vulnerable animals; lost and scared
Some alone and some paired

Finding tremendous treatments to eliminate viruses
Reminding us that hospitals are doing what they can to care
for us

A cleaner environment will reduce all harsh bacteria that is
in the air
Stupendous flower beds held in allotments
Bees swooping amongst the greenery
They are fairies searching for magical dust
Pollinating the world, they are the ones we entrust.

Please note with care
Care suggests compliments, actions, words and attention
If we use care in our world we will be left with joy, happiness
and trust
Care is holding the key, to all good.

Zoe McKenzie (12)
Gosford Hill School, Kidlington

Human

The human race
Humans, that's us
Me and you
Race, it's what we all do

We try to win
But only end up falling back
But as long as you know how, what, why, when, where and who
You have a lot more ahead of you than just a race

How did you get where you are?
What do you get from this?
Why are you still racing?
When did it start?

Where will it end?
And
Most importantly
Who will you be at the end?

Me
My answers are simple
How did I get where I am?
Society opened a tunnel and I crawled through

What do I get from this?
Nothing, just more social points

Why am I still racing?
I don't know, I honestly couldn't tell you

When did it start?
When society grew big enough to drag me down with it
Where will it end?
Here, now

And
Most importantly
Who will I be in the end?
I will still be me, just higher up the social scale

After all these questions are asked
And you've stopped racing
I could then proudly say
I am part of the human race

The human race
Is wonderful
And not as hard as it seems
Because of you and me

The human race
Humans, that's us
Me and you
Race is what we all used to do.

Kayleigh Harmsworth (13)
Gosford Hill School, Kidlington

Differences

Grapes. People
There are green and red grapes
There are black and white people
There are different colours in the rainbow
And there are different colours in the human race

So let's just stop selling red grapes
Because they are a different colour, because that's fair
Isn't it?
There are different colours all around you
So why can't some people accept that there's
White and black people in the human race?

People laugh at the word 'gay' as if there's
Something wrong with it
People laugh when someone says
'You're bent,' like there's something wrong with it
But they never laugh at, 'You're not gay.'
They say it as if it's an insult
So the next insult is, 'You're not,' is it?
Is it meant to be offensive or is it meant to be
A statement
Because it's funny, is it?
Being different from everyone else is funny

Or maybe it's funny because the person
Saying it, doesn't want to be
Different and wants to be the same
Boring person that every one of
Their friends is
Or maybe because
They are scared to be different!
Well guess what?
You can start being different by
Not laughing at those stupid statements
Because they are not funny.

Erin Mitchell (12)
Gosford Hill School, Kidlington

Tears Of Fears

It's the way the dark scares people at night
It sounds like they're being plundered by a knife
Parents come to them
Only to sing a lullaby
It feels good to know your fears
The only time you think you don't
Is when you and your mates have had a few beers
You're diving home
Just to say hi to your mum
She offers you a cup of tea
You turn around and say you've got to flee
You go back to the car you call a she
You put your foot down and go above 90 on a freeway
You see a cat crossing the road
So you swerve and then hit a curb
You flip over the railing and crash into a pond
You say to yourself, 'That's another fear gone.'
The one of being set on fire
The sound of the ambulance ringing in your ears
You're laying in a bed in the JR
And then you remember your one big fear
Having the feeling of maybe dying
You think of your mum
And how she offered you some tea
And how this could've been avoided

You take your last breath
Whilst you hold your mum's hand
You hear the beat of your heart getting slower
And then it happens, the long treacherous beep
You see a bright light and then notice a large stairway
You get to a gate and right there and then
Your life has come to a very dead end...

Alfie Wall (13)
Gosford Hill School, Kidlington

The Power Of Love

Love is not a game or a challenging chore
It's a special bond where you're not just friends any more
No money, no prizes, no rewards are earned
If you're doing it for that then you should be concerned

Love makes you laugh when you want to cry
And it makes you live when you want to die
Makes you smile when you want to run for miles
Trying to find another lover but knowing deep down
That there isn't another who loves you as much
Who puts up with your complaints and feels your pain

The amount of love is unquantifiable for the truth is
undeniable
That as long as you've got each other
You don't need money and cute bunnies or a Lamborghini
That serves you honey or the rich smell of roses and selfie
poses
That you can post on your Instagram and make yourself
noticed

Love is the strongest power in the world
More fierce than lightning
More precious that pearls
Anyone that knows love knows that it never accepts a
defeat
Because it will keep fighting and fighting until there is
nothing else to eat

So never ever mess with love
Instead treat it like a baseball glove
For it protects from the ball of pain and sorrow
And catches it like there's no tomorrow.

Joseph Philippe Hichens (13)
Gosford Hill School, Kidlington

She Still Remembers

Wind whispers; a few leaves left my mango trees
My mango trees are always surrounded by those noisy bees
It shall be the season for mangoes soon, I thought
As I tie my memories into a knot
When they came and took me back on my favourite spot
Behind the branches and hard to be seen
I just sat there, watched
Watched the passengers hurry, the shopkeepers furried
Watched my time pass by...
How old are you? I asked, my tree just smiled, refused to speak
But in a sudden, the cloud started to leak
I knew I must be on my way
Will you be here on the next day?
I heard a voice murmur, but not clear so I didn't reply
How I left without any words of goodbye
Left with an osmanthus' sweet scent and golden mangoes
Though I didn't know
This will be my last chance, to share my secrets and his mangoes

She still remembers a girl under some mango trees
As she grew, less and less time spent with her favourite tree
Until there was no time
She left, never came back
Maybe there is no point for going back to see some ordinary mango trees

Or she is just too scared to face an empty wasteland
With not even one mark for the mango trees that occupied
her whole childhood.

Yanglan Smith (13)
Gosford Hill School, Kidlington

Growing Up

Growing up is a big part of life
We follow our dreams
With people by our sides
And try to live our lives to the extremes

At five a girl wanted to fly
She sat by her window dreaming every night
Everyone told her she couldn't
But that night she shut her eyes and took flight

At eight a girl wanted to dance
She watched everyone else do it
She tripped, she stumbled
But she got back up again and never quit

At twelve a girl wanted to be a footballer
Everyone told her that it was for only for boys
She practised every day after school
She joined a team and she was overjoyed

At sixteen a girl wanted to pass her GCSEs
A teacher called her dumb
So she went home and studied
And she proved him wrong

At eighteen a girl wanted to graduate
To make her family proud
A student made fun of her
But her name was read aloud

At twenty-five a girl wanted to get married
Her colleagues told her to dream on
But soon she whispered, 'I do'
She thought her childhood was gone

Your childhood will forever be in your heart
So long as you will never part.

Abigail Strauther (12)
Gosford Hill School, Kidlington

Oxygen Debt

Cold
Cold feet, cold nose, cold ears
Crunch, crunch, crunch
That is the sound of cold feet on frost

Left, right, left
The pattern of strides going across
Across frost and grass and road
Past forest, past town, past house and field

The burning of your legs
The left, right, left becomes
Left, right, left, right, left

Though the gnarling teeth of winter bites
The fire in your lungs, throat and legs burn on

The heat rises, the cold blows
The running of your nose
The running of your feet that go
Left, right, left
Crunch, crunch, crunch
That's the sound of frost under frozen feet

Thinking, thinking of nothing but the cold and the burning
And the weight in your chest that you heave
Every time you breath the weight gets
Heavier, heavier, heavier still

Until you can hear the blood pound in your ears
B-bom, b-bom, b-bom

The faster, faster you run
The more fire in your lungs
The more burning in your legs
And the heaving of your chest
Until *b-bom, b-bom, b-bom*
You stop
In oxygen debt.

Amelie Prior (13)
Gosford Hill School, Kidlington

Nope

What is it about these religious extremists?
Why do they do it?
These people are taking their lives and others
When the children die, think of their fathers and mothers
When they strike, your lives flash before your eyes
Looking down at all of those poor lost lives
But if you are one of the lucky people
You won't stop feeling weak and feeble

So maybe...
Is it because they were told to do it?
No one knows really
But all we want for our country
Is for it to stop
Why do they do it? I mean
Our lives are put in danger
Because of some stranger
Although not really a stranger to some
No one knows where they are
Whether they be near or far

Who knows where they hide
Because they could be your neighbour on the left hand side
Who knows when they will strike?
It's so unpredictable they could even explode on a bike!

But what will happen to us and our town?
Because the more this happens, the more people wear a
frown

So please, we ask for a little hope
That when we ask, 'Will they do it again?'
The answer will simply be
'Nope.'

Amy Neale (13)
Gosford Hill School, Kidlington

Bullying

Bullying
It pulls you down
And you can never push yourself off the ground
You're two-faced, you're a bore, you don't matter any more

These are the things that are sad
When you cry so hard but you're ignored
You're as lonely as air, I can tell you're afraid
'Go burn in Hell,' they say

After all that has happened you just
Snap! You tend to fight back
They try to break you and that is that

If you don't tell it keeps on going
The fear, the pain, the depression
You won't be able to run or hide
You just stand in the open and hear the laughing
The mockery that makes you cry
The darkness in their souls
And they just stand by

And the world starts to crumble and
You just can't stand it and then
You feel as if everyone hates you and that you're coming to
an end
And you fall
And you're no more

But once you tell, they help
They fight back and with that the bullies step back
Take a chance and tell
Sooner or later they're old news
And remember, bullies are always jealous of you.

Faith Lily Turner (13)
Gosford Hill School, Kidlington

Change

Earth is a huge museum
Full of beautiful things
Each made to make you feel something
Maybe it's the snow
Lit dimly with a soft yellow light
Maybe it's the eyes of the one you love
Maybe,
Maybe it's just the art
Maybe we were all placed here to see this museum
This work of art
Ever changing
Maybe we weren't supposed to touch or talk
Just appreciate for a short time...
But we touched
And we talked
And we ruined this work of art
We ruined this museum
We edited and ruined this place we call home
You take a walk
You come across a forest
A beautiful place
Well, it was you see
But your tired eyes change the view
To butterflies with broken wings
And frosty, dull, dying trees

You feel your pulse quicken
And the panic building in your heart
But you stand there motionless
Just staring at this work of art
You feel a tear drop leave your eye
And at the same time, a teardrop falls from the sky
It was a beautiful place you see
But your hands moulded it into a certain shape
Easier on your eyes, but harder to create.

Paige Simpson (13)
Gosford Hill School, Kidlington

Selfish Society

Enjoy your time in society
Your only time is right now!
We promise to respect you
If you're not always so blue
Your personalty isn't a problem
Or I will move on if you're such a boredom
I am going to love your looks
That is, unless you're into books

Society is like a monster, lurking in the shadows
Waiting to grab you and bring you right down
Our world is pretty ugly
Society is defined as a dove
Peace and gentility...
In reality, it's a glove
It hides our beauty within; where it can't be seen to be
destroyed
But shows our unique features to be judged

Society will bring you down
For the simplest of characteristics we were made to love
Society brings you sinking until you reach the bottom of the
sea
And you feel you're not worth it
We feel the delicate water run down our cheeks

Drip, drip...
But you just have to swim to the surface and stand strong

However, when you hurt society
You have others to blame
But you should realise
Importantly, society is you...

Tia Celina Hussain (13)
Gosford Hill School, Kidlington

My Son, My Son

My son, my son
Come and sit with me
I have a story about a boy called John
Who was just like you and me

His eyes shone brighter than the stars
And his heart made everyone happy
He believed in equal rights
Believing this gave him terrible frights

My son, my son
His country was not like ours
If you say something they don't agree with
You shall be behind bars

He ran down the corridors in all directions
All he found was imperfection

His family were taken out of the cell
And then they were tortured to fiery hell

My son, my son
Don't take this for granted
These horrible tortures have not ended

My son, my son
I will tell you about another boy
Who was in a similar situation
But in another place

This place was a labyrinth of endless despair
No heavenly houses, just old buildings of a nightmare
He said something similar to the other boy John
But his life was taken unlike John's.

Joshua Hedges (13)
Gosford Hill School, Kidlington

Same

Life
It's like a box of chocolates
Melt-in-the-mouth, scrumptious chocolates
Milk, white or dark
All leave you with the same spark
They're beautiful, delicious
And importantly, all equal
Just like all human people

It's like some souls
Just love to be cold
Love to be racist
Fancy being prejudiced?

Use someone's colour
To be an oppressor?
Use someone's religion
As an excuse to eliminate them?
Use someone's race
To mess up their darn face?

Why do we not accept an African
Just because they're 'a black one'?
Why are they all the same
Even tough terrorists only think they are sane?
Why evict just one type of country
Even though all of them have some of that conviction?

Stop
Contemplate
You're just the same. Like the chocolates
No matter the colour
The race
The religion
Really. We're all the same. We are human
No matter what differences we contain.

Tim Millard (13)
Gosford Hill School, Kidlington

Everyone Is Different...

Everyone is different
Weight, body size, physical disability
Other peoples' perception
Could change someone's life

Everyone is different
Anorexia, anxiety, depression
Why do I look in the mirror
When it can change my life

Everyone is different
Feeling so left out, so-called
Friends back-stabbing
Self-harm is my punishment

Everyone is different
If you're small or if you're tall
I have been told a million times
Size is not everything

Everyone is different
Some are brainier than others
But neither should be punished by so called mates
Who see you as a threat

Everyone is different
Black or white, it shouldn't matter
But it really does in some peoples' eyes
Why is a person judged by their cover?

Everyone is different
Weight, body size, physical disability
The colour of skin
Each of these could end a life.

Thara Parthipan (13)

Gosford Hill School, Kidlington

Cruel To Be Kind

I am a fish in a sea of monsters
The world at my feet but I'm running away
Running like a blade cutting through ice, skating quicker
and faster
To keep at the top, *flash!*
It's over
The moment disappeared

I am the greatest
I will go far
Is what I tell myself
Every day I tell this to me

It may be cruel to be kind
But everyone must be cruel sometimes

The wind whispers to me
Telling me the good and the bad
The right and the wrong

Which one to listen to
I listen to the loudest
They say the loudest is the worst

But who cares!
Who really, really cares?
No one

People's hearts can be as cold as ice
Frost bitten, cold and dark
Although warm and fluid
Like an ocean
Flowing and crashing

It's OK to be cruel
But they just can't find out...
It was
You!

Maisey Fielder (13)
Gosford Hill School, Kidlington

The Final Poem

I walked along the sandy beach
Waves coming, to and fro
I ran right through the countryside
Winds flowing, back and forth

And then I went
Through the city, through the wood
Full of pity
Running, running as fast as I could

Full of pity
For those who run
Running, running
As fast as they can
Through streets, through towns
Through paths, through alleys
Past dogs and hounds, through hills or valleys

And when we stop running
Will this be over...

Will we rot away, like fallen trees
Will our hearts keep running when they're released?
When we just lay there, like a sleeping bear
Will our minds run free, with a new found flare...

Running, running, until we drop
Will we fade away; or stay and play?

And although we may not know today
We keep running, running, until we drop
But our humanity will never stop.

Emily Beckley (13)
Gosford Hill School, Kidlington

Untitled

I long to see the light again
Each day gets harder and harder
To pass, like heavy stones balancing
On my two weak shoulders

Every single day they start to argue
I long to see them get along again
Each argument is a waterfall bursting out
About about to flood
When will this stop!

When I saw them get married
I knew they made a perfect fit
Such as cheese and a burger
And they did for a while

It's like a car on a motorway
It speeds up fast
And when it runs out of petrol
It stops all of a sudden

The edges of constant arguments
Often a short while
They had you divorced
I was glad, mad, guilty, shallow

Each tear had fallen from my eye
It felt like I was in deep water

That night I couldn't sleep
I was worried about everything
And that was one of the quietest nights of my life!

Alice Pricope (13)
Gosford Hill School, Kidlington

Not Alone

Children have been captured
Stuck in the middle of these awful zones
Can't sleep at night, too scared of war
Throughout history this has been the world's downpour

They can't go home any more
Stuck in these awful camps
Nobody will open their door
Nobody cares for others any more

Race, culture, background or size
It shouldn't matter
We are all the same
Who wants to be in pain?
Just watching them out there, unable to help
It's enough to drive anybody insane

It's as though it's a board game
And we're all tiny pieces being moved around helplessly
Why can't we make a stand, choose when or what to fight
Whatever happened to the human right?

We're all supporting you out here
You just need to know that you're not alone
If only the clock could go back
Then they could get their lives back on track...

Adam James Blake (13)
Gosford Hill School, Kidlington

Never Be Gone Too Far

You reach out and grab my hand
Knowing it's the last time I still stand
Here, where the memories are at their finest
But know I'll never be gone too far

I watch the smile fall off your face
As I waste time staring back
To you where I always meant to be
Just know I'll never be gone too far

Now you must stay stuck here
While I fly free from this prison
Leaving you some of the best times
With the rest for you to make
It's a chance that I will take
To watch you make the rest of your story
Trapped between these sorry walls
Please know I'll never be gone too far

Just promise you'll never forget
That if my skies have turned sin black
I'll always look back up to you
Laid free shining in the clouds
Where we're proud to be who we are
Where we'll never be gone too far.

Holly Hunt (13)
Gosford Hill School, Kidlington

An Online Lifetime

I'm here to tell a story
One on a present theme
Of an 'online lifetime'
Where all eyes meet a screen

In this online world
Where everything is shared
Facebook, Snapchat, Twitter
We should be running scared

We have to look our best
For a life full of hate
Laughs behind backs, rude comments
Where no one changes fate

Barely any feelings
We keep them all inside
We are a crying baby, when we lose the Internet
Without a phone, we cannot even go outside

No one dares to read a book
From years ago, a time that saw a change
A time so close, yet so far away
An important time, yet to us so strange

Oh and he looks down upon us
In the happy place, so colourful and bright
The light, the home of all things good
That happy place is slipping slowly out of sight.

Erin Grace Pittuck (12)
Gosford Hill School, Kidlington

Terrorism

When it happens it is not a good sight
You know that it is not right
It could happen at any time
When it does it's a shock
It will cause the Earth to rock
It could be a case of wrong time, wrong place
It even could be about race
You know the mum will cry
And 'cause of this you'll know why
Walking along without a care
The man with the gun will he dare
Bang! Bang! from his gun
The man with the gun is now on the run
And the door snarled at what the man had done
He gulped down some pride
Now he is looking for his ride
Screaming streets filled with fear
The man with the gun, is he near?
'For Syria, Islamic State will fight.'
London, will you sleep tonight?
Gun men falling to the ground
Policemen running all around
The fight on terror will carry on
Let's stand together, we will have won.

Jonathan Forse (13)
Gosford Hill School, Kidlington

Anxiety

You smile
Because if you don't you'll break
Thoughts screaming
In your head until it aches

You weep
Alone in your room you cry
Sitting lonely and terrified
Because this is more than just shy

You try
To talk but can't get the words out
Feels like nobody understands
How you can be so petrified with doubt

You lie
Awake at night
The clock glares at you from the shelf
Getting to sleep is a fight

You stand
In front of the mirror
Checking your face to see if
You can go out without feeling terror

You smile
But this time it's real
Yes, there's something wrong with your brain
But you know that you're loved

And appreciated
By so many
And it doesn't matter if you look OK
Because you are amazing.

Susannah Willis (13)
Gosford Hill School, Kidlington

Respect

You crawl, you walk, you run and cry
But the main point of this is to never die

Respect

The war begins
You fight, you kill, hearing deafening rings

Respect

I hope, I pray and refuse to lose
Even though God's always on the move

Respect

You feel down, you feel loved
Even though you can feel your heart being crushed

Respect

Respect is key
But it's not about me

Respect

When you're in the dark, never be scared
That's what parents should always declare

Respect
You graze your knee but it's not about me
When you're sobbing for help
When all you want is a warm rug

Respect
When someone comes along to give you
The biggest of hugs.

Jack Ward (12)
Gosford Hill School, Kidlington

Lost And Found

Its OK my child, for you'll see
Me in a while, wait for me
On the other side
And I'll sing you a lullaby

There were all around screams
And everyone were at their knees
One by one they pushed on
As they fought to take the transport

Women and men were left behind
As children got a free ride
Grenades all around went off
The men and woman dropped

It's OK my child, for you'll see
Me in a while, wait for me
On the other side
And I'll sing you a lullaby

We will wait for all of you
And if not you've died
And I'll have to sing myself a lullaby

It's OK my child, for you'll see
Me in a while, wait for me
On the other side
And I'll sing you a lullaby.

Kieran Blackwood (13)
Gosford Hill School, Kidlington

My Life

I was born on the 15th of February 2004
Luckily I didn't get left at a door
Said my first word when I was one
And luckily my dad hadn't gone

Made my first steps at two
So I learnt what to do
Got stitches at three
Because of a bumblebee

Went to school at four
And Mum cried when she left me at the door
Started to play rugby by five
And I really enjoyed scoring tries

Had to go up the stairs in school at seven
It was nice and bright like Heaven
When I was leaving school and got people to sign my shirt
But it was a lot of work

Life can be amazing like me enjoying mine
All you have to do it try and make it that way
Sometimes you even get signs
And some people do that by just wearing a hat.

Jack McGrory Foord (13)
Gosford Hill School, Kidlington

Just Say No!

Don't give in to people saying,
'Hey, have this, try that.'
Don't let people make you eat and drink
The things you shouldn't be

Those people that you call your friends clearly aren't that loyal
They tell you what to do and be
And make you a different person
There are plenty of people to support you

You come home upset from school
From people calling names
For saying no to that one thing
How unfair is that?

If you become the bigger person
And stand up for yourself
They too will say it's wrong
And you were right all along

That sip of alcohol or that cigarette you decided not to have
Could be the best choice that you ever made
So make your life a little longer
And just say no!

Louise Kate Akers (13)
Gosford Hill School, Kidlington

Sweet Nothings

Whisper sweet nothings into my ear
It's all I need to hear
It comes from the heart
Sometimes you don't know where to start
You say you'll be there through every single emotion
You say you'll be there with all your love and devotion
You say you'll be there to guide us through every storm
You say you'll be there when I call

Whisper sweet nothings into my ear
It's all I need to hear
It comes from every direction
So thankful for that, it's such a blessing
You say I should pick up my phone at a quarter to three
You say you'll be at my back door in your skinny white jeans
You say you'll be taking your chances
Maybe this time there will be more dances
Whisper sweet nothings into my ear
It's all I need to hear.

Bethany Samuel (13)
Gosford Hill School, Kidlington

Is She Really Happy?

Is she really happy
Or is that just how it seems?
When the sky is so high above her
Is she the only one to hear her scream?
Is she really happy
Or is that just how it seems?
When she falls apart every day
Due to broken beams
Is she really happy
Or is that just how it seems?
When the loneliness only ever fades
When she's lost far in her dreams
Is she really happy
Or is that just how it seems?
When society taught everyone
To lower their self-esteem
Is she really happy
Or is that just how it seems?
When the shadows cover up her face
So no one can see her tears go downstream
Is she really happy
Or is that just how it seems?
When she's never even seen
How, even through the darkness, her smile still seems to gleam.

Ewelina Sobon (13)
Gosford Hill School, Kidlington

I Wish You Were Here

I wish you were here
With all the smiles you make
You twist my head and make it shake
But most of all I love you

You've told me not to make foolish mistakes
And not to take risks that I wanted to take
You were always there when I needed you

I know you're not with the family any more
But my heart is with you no matter what
I will take your place and do everyone proud
Without you by my side

I miss you on family meet ups
When everyone drinks and chats
Including when Tim does the BBQ
And the burgers end up flat

I wish you were here
Everyone has a beer during a cheer
To say that we are thankful for you to be part of our family
And that we love you, Richard!

Katie-Louise Curry (13)
Gosford Hill School, Kidlington

My Poem

Police
They should bring peace
Not hate
Because if I had to give it a rate
4 1/2

They are stereotypical 95% of the time
Especially when it comes to crime
This shouldn't happen
Whether you're man or woman

Police
They should bring peace
Not hate
Because if I had to give it a rate
4 1/2
This happened to me
I got put under arrest
I was sad and didn't agree
But I'm lucky I didn't object

I felt like a speck of salt
Surrounded with others
This felt like everything came to a halt
This made the front covers
Police
They should bring peace
Not hate

Because if I had to give it a rate
4 1/2.

Alfie Cripps (13)
Gosford Hill School, Kidlington

Society

We blame society for a lot, famine, war and last but not least, pain
The truth is we all contribute to that, we all have argued
Or are arguing with someone about something
Sometimes, not always, but in the end
It creates a malicious war
We waste food all the time, thus creating famine

Pain. Pain comes in all shapes and sizes
Just like people, but no matter how big or small
it still hurts, pain will always have an impact on people
Whether it means crying or getting revenge
Just like it does on society

We continue to blame society for all that is wrong with the world
Neglecting the fact that most of it is our fault
So continue to blame society but just remember
You're a part of society too.

India Nayyar (13)
Gosford Hill School, Kidlington

Motorbikes

Biking through the grey dark track
The bikes passing around
100mph, taking the first lean
Scorching of the exhaust breaking eardrums

If I fall
I will get back up
I will never stay falling
If I lie down
I will pick myself up
If I lose the handle bars
I will take control
And carry on

Forget the glass slippers, this girl wears motorbike boots
Never look back
Believe in yourself
Don't wear a crown
Live your life through the eyes of a helmet
Live your life on a bike

I have the best bike
The bike roars like a lion as you rev the ferocious engine
The lion is searching for its prey
As it is searching around the bend
Angry as an Alaskan husky.

Ellie Anderson (13)
Gosford Hill School, Kidlington

Jacob's Ladder

Look up and around
Don't miss a sound
Take in the sight
Watch the birds take flight

Enjoy, have fun, now make good choices
Trickling water sounds like voices
Thudding feet leap from rock to rock
The birds fly high in their flock

Caught by the wind the T-shirts fly
When you reach the top you'll heave a sigh
Ice-cold water gives you shocks
Surrounding you are warm mossy rocks

Watch as the rocks merge into dead grass
And the fluffy clouds as they float past
Animal odour surrounds you
That doesn't stop you from enjoying the view

Look up and around
Don't miss a sound
Take in the sight
Watch the birds take flight.

Georgia Jenkins (14)
Gosford Hill School, Kidlington

Classical Music

The sounds of nature
Ring with their music
The wind, the leaves
The birds, and the trees

The sounds of the orchestra
Sing with their music
The brass, the cello
The percussion and the oboe

The sound of the choir
Bring us their music
The tenors, the altos
The basses and the sopranos

But the sounds of electricity
Lead with their music
The volume, the screeching
The bashing, and the beeping

The sounds of classical music
The deepness and beauty
The sounds of popular music
The shallowness and noise

Which one is better
The former or the latter?
Of course, it's the first one
Classical music.

David Willis (13)
Gosford Hill School, Kidlington

Dan The Man

Dan the man
Has got a plan
And that's it
He lives in his van
Drives around all day
Or sits in the park

He wears the same clothes every day
As he can't afford to buy more
Everyone judges him
Calls him a tramp
Fills his day with shouts of,
'Oi, weirdo.'

But Dan's just a man
No one knows anything about him or his past
He's never met his dad
His mum
Terminally ill
But he's got no money to pay the bill

So he sold his house
All his possessions
Just to help his mum
She lives in the back
And he nurses her
But no one knows

But after all
Dan
Is still just a man.

Henry Mimpress (13)
Gosford Hill School, Kidlington

I Will Always Remember...

I've known her all my life
I remember the days where we played
Went shopping and just enjoyed life

Everyone was happy until
Until we found out
Found out that she had cancer
She had cancer but still lived
Lived her life but just a little different

I remember I went to visit her
I sat beside her
Smiled
I remembered the day she came home
The day she sadly died
I remember those days well

All the memories I will remember
And that day in November
Where she died but flew up to the sky
Where it was better for her
But I will always remember
The happy memories and the tough times
I will always remember her and her smile.

Katelyn Worvill (12)
Gosford Hill School, Kidlington

The Streets Of Shadows

Mobs and gangs
Dogs bearing fangs
Alcohol and drugs
Alleyways filled with thugs
Bear claws
How many laws
Are going to be broken?
This neighbourhood
Home of the hood
Children being raised
While being illegal is a craze
Can't go out at night
Without seeing a fight
It's not right
Being a child should be a fun time
Where everyone is so, so kind
Not guns, drugs and quitters
Shouldn't have dead little sisters
Shouldn't be home alone
Your parents starve you to the bone
This might seem like dystopia to you
But in some places it's a reality
Be thankful for what you've got
Because this lot
Their souls are about to rot.

Tom Evans (13)
Gosford Hill School, Kidlington

Life

Vishnu very vaguely victorious
My brain is like a pick-and-mix box
Full of thoughts bursting out like a volcano erupting
It is full of whooshing power of a wind turbine trumpeting at speed
With these thoughts, I maximise my brain capacity
Including effective equation and wonderful words
I am an Indian who likes to play cricket
I thwack the ball with tremendous power like the Hulk
Running like Usain Bolt
Could see fielders chasing the ball
Could hear the stumping footsteps as the ball is thrown
With the whoosh of the ball gliding through the air
It felt like a giant was about to step on me as I was wondering
If the ball had hit the stumps.

Vishnu Ganesh (13)
Gosford Hill School, Kidlington

The Highs And Woes Of The NHS

For hundreds of years medical care was only available to
the few.
Not the many.
The many couldn't afford this most essential of essentials
And then
In 1948
The National Health Service was born.

Now the many could have the same healthcare as the few,
Until Jeremy Hunt came along.
Budget cut after budget cut came
As blow after blow rained down
Less staff,
Less beds,
Less medicine,
Cuts, cuts and more cuts
A never-ending stream of cuts.

No pay rises,
No over-time pay,
No nothing for the many.
And what will become of the NHS?
It will be non-existent soon.

Alex McCluskey (13)
Gosford Hill School, Kidlington

Lost And Not Found

How does it feel?
To be alone
To feel lost
Lost and not found

When nobody's around you
You're in a room on your own
It's dark and foggy
And the door is closed

Your cheeks feel wet
There's a puddle on the floor
Your eyes are burning
Drip, drip, drip

You're upset, confused, angry
You don't know which way to go
Or who to talk to
Who can you trust?

You want to find that door
Open it up
Find someone
Cry on their shoulder
But no one's there
For as far as the eye can see.

Katie Parsons (13)
Gosford Hill School, Kidlington

Grampy

On New Year's Eve 2015, everything was fine
In Ipswich with my auntie and cousins playing in the sunlight
A few hours later just before tea, my aunt went to see
If my gramp was in need
My aunt was rushing down the street for help
Her boyfriend went to see
When they were talking I heard them saying that my gramp
had fallen asleep
My dad found out a few minutes later, he cried in shock
And said, 'I will speak to you later.'
My gramp is in a better place now
Watching upon us with a smile on his face
Saying, 'I am peaceful that I achieved the age of 66.'

Harvey Mark Winterbourne (13)
Gosford Hill School, Kidlington

Colours

Colours of grey enlighten the world I live in
Memories of you seem to creep around the corners of my mind
Endless thoughts and images of you haunt me every time I hear your name
Overwhelming emotion my body can't contain
It fills me with unbearable anger and the pain you gave to my family
You left me when I was only two and never turned to say goodbye
I forget all about you as I grew
I went to school then became distressed
As everything went, I became a mess
The day I realised he didn't love me
For if he did, he would've stayed.

Caitlin Maison (13)
Gosford Hill School, Kidlington

Prisoner Of War

Come sit, my little one
Let me tell you how people are
When wars start with greed
And how concealed lies char

For she died, in war
In hunger and pain
Since when have we said never again?
In books, on shelves
In laws by fame
Helping no one is like a chain

Why truth will slaughter
And discrimination is pride
How with untouched eyes my daughter
Will watch blankly inside

So come sit, my little one
Let me tell you how people are
How prisoner of war
Is what we are.

Arta Preteni (13)
Gosford Hill School, Kidlington

Growing Up

You go from five and chasing butterflies
The dress up into princess costumes
And the playing with dolls

Then suddenly you become a teenager
You have all these responsibilities

You don't know how to handle them
Arguing with Mum, arguing with Dad

Those good days and them bad days
The boyfriends, the relationships

Why did we want to grow up?
Who told us it was this hard...

All the responsibilities
All the hard work
Never grow up.

Eloise Annabel Potter (13)
Gosford Hill School, Kidlington

Hidden Talent

She lives in a shack
In darkness in black
Her voice is the light
To guide her in the night

Is she one of those people
Who keep their mouths shut
And they keep in the light
So very secure and tight

I wish one day she would speak
To see what a great person she could be
But all hidden up inside
Like a snail who wants to hide

I will try to guide her out of the night
As we will proceed into humanity
Leaving the past behind
It's just you and I.

Jayden Baskerville (12)
Gosford Hill School, Kidlington

Gramp

Gramp, you were loving and caring
You were kind and amazing
But the birds will continue to sing

Gramp, you were knowledgeable and talented
You were helpful and cheerful
Until my world exploded

Gramp, you were thoughtful and brave
You were generous and perfect as could be

You were my hero and life saver
You were the greatest gramp
Any gramp could be

You were more than my gramp
You were one of my best friends
To everyone, not just me.

Jade Loder (13)
Gosford Hill School, Kidlington

YNWA

Up the stairs and into the kop
All the players warming up
Jurgen eagerly watching by the side
Lions running on the wide
All the kop on full force like a giant wave of red
'You'll never walk alone,' is the noise
Hendo leading out the boys
Coutinho goes and scores a goal, all the players screaming,
'Roar!'
The team a pack of lions, 4-0, Origi golden goals galore
The stadium, the fans' home, all welcome, why can't we
stay?
Waiting to go back another day.

Tom Underwood (13)

Gosford Hill School, Kidlington

Untitled

The world is full of so much hatred
For example, YouTube comments lately.
Telling someone 'Kill yourself'
Really can't be good for mental health

Racist stereotypes
aimed at someone campaigning for their rights
they're uncalled for
It's like people try to start their own war

Won't you look around and see
they're just like you, just like me
just because their skin colour doesn't match yours
or maybe just because they're poor
you don't have to hate them
you just have to embrace them.

Lorcan Johnston-Smyth (13)
Gosford Hill School, Kidlington

Differences

Everyone's different in their own special way
No one is known to be the same
From race to religion
To gender to trait
Piece by piece not every puzzle fits
The only way is to accept the differences

Some people are selfish, mean and harsh
And others may have a good, great heart
Because something may have happened within their past
But the people who are selfish, mean and harsh
Just stop!
Before time flies past...
Tick!
Tock!

Amber Parker (12)
Gosford Hill School, Kidlington

Don't Have A Title

I'm too tired of being hated
I'm too tired to wake
I hate the way I look
I'm so tired of people giving me sympathy
That's why I keep causing infamy
To keep the people between you and me
But I can't stop causing the sorrows between you and me
That's why I keep falling to my knees when I think of you and me
But now I'm too tired to even joke about you and me
So that's why I keep writing these symphonies
To keep the peace between you and me.

Sam Pitts
Gosford Hill School, Kidlington

Diamond Island

Waking up to the smell of pandesal
Coming from the dining table
So heavenly
The noise of goats and horses
Neigh, neigh, everything around me I recognised
It was my home
My diamond island
The scent, scene and sound fades
As I hear a roar
From a beast pulling me
Back to reality
Ring, ring, trying to suppress the noise
Trying to anchor myself
Back to my precious island
Everything I do fails
Another day in England.

Julian Quinola (12)
Gosford Hill School, Kidlington

Feeling Left Out

Why is it always me?
I have no friends any more
It's so unfair
I can't do this

I feel so depressed
I think it's the way I dress
But no one is impressed
So I may change

It maybe just be the way I act
But it may not be
If you don't try things
You will never find out

This is what happens when you try
I have more friends now
I help people that don't
I take pride of myself.

Samuel Stowell (13)
Gosford Hill School, Kidlington

Ode To My Parents

Most wonderful, most marvellous
I cherish you
Always there when I need you
A call, a text
You are by my side

From the moment I was born
You were there comforting me
You've taught me how to live, laugh and love
The people that surround me

I have grown to my full potential
Learnt to motivate myself at school
And enjoy the outside, with family and friends
Because of you

Because of you, I am who I am
Me.

Lucy Bryant (13)
Gosford Hill School, Kidlington

Football Poem

Whoa! As I play my team game
Saving the goals
Then my teammate scores
The winning goal

The crowds cheering are as
Loud as lions roaring
The atmosphere is rising

The referee blows his mighty whistle
Telling us it's offside

I wonder who is gong to win
The brilliant game
The crowd is screaming
As I save the goals
Football is like life, it requires hard work
Dedication and respect.

Isabel Emptage (13)
Gosford Hill School, Kidlington

Bullying

Bullies are not big, they're just mean
Trying to make you small
They try to hurt your feelings
Even if you're at home or school
Trying to bring you down

People stay at home, afraid because of bullies
It's like they're alone
They depress you, it's not funny, stop now
You're not funny, it's not nice
Now they're afraid at night

Bullying kills and killing can come from bullying.

Tom Daniel Merrill (12)
Gosford Hill School, Kidlington

Ode To My Goalpost

You're always by my side
My saviour, my defender
Saving my honour as a goalie
Keeping our team's winning streak
Keeping us in the game
No matter what hits, you're still
The 5ft beast that stands strong
There may be another person between the sticks
But I know you'll do just the same for them
I want you there, almost as much as I need you there
To save the top corner curler
That I can't quite reach yet.

Archie Pepper (13)
Gosford Hill School, Kidlington

Thugs, Mugs, Bugs

Thugs, mugs, bugs
Like creepy-crawlies
They climb
Through windows
Through doors
Breaking laws
Like chores

No police
No control
Like living
In a hellhole
In the dark
All alone
Pleading that
They will go

Out my house
Down the street
To where
All the others meet
Share their goods
Go back to the woods
To sleep
And leave my town to weep.

Tom Scaife (12)
Gosford Hill School, Kidlington

Art

Gripping the brush
As colour splashes to and fro
Blues, reds, yellows! Filling the page
Taste of paint covering my face
Sound of sweet birds ringing in my ear
Summer sun beaming through the windowpane
My mind concentrating carefully with every detail
Drip, drop
Drip, drop
Water droplets rolling off the paper onto the dusty
floorboards
Moment caught on canvas, frozen in time.

Sophie Port (13)
Gosford Hill School, Kidlington

Sports

Sport is wonderful
From the swimming pool to the football pitch
There isn't anything sport can't give
The squelching, the splashing, the booing and the cheer
That happens in a tier

Supporters scream, 'Ref!'
As if there was a theft
When injuries are bad
Everyone goes mad
Players slipping, sliding, skidding around
Eventually they'll end up on the ground.

Harrison Bates (13)
Gosford Hill School, Kidlington

Football

Football is the best sport you can play in the day
And night with the sunlight
And the darkness of the night

Benfica has the Black Panther
Eusebio is loved in every country he played
For Benfica for his 21st birthday he played
Until the darkness of the night

Benfica, my dream team
I would love to play from the sunlight
To the darkness of the night.

Francisco Neves (12)
Gosford Hill School, Kidlington

Growing Up

What I love about growing up is making friends
What I hate about friends is not all of them stay
What I love about growing up is society
What I hate about society is having to be a certain way
What I love about growing up is family
What I hate about family is arguments
What I love about growing up is having your own identity
What I hate about identity is people judge the way you look
or act.

Tayla Alice Kuhne (13)
Gosford Hill School, Kidlington

Hate

You don't even need a gun
You don't even need a pill
If you ever wanna die
Fall in love and
You get killed

Getting in a fight
From what you look like
To your voice and body
Trying to bounce back
It is hard to know you're under attack

Sticks and stones
Won't break your bones
But words will always
Hurt you.

Sarah Cooper (13)
Gosford Hill School, Kidlington

You Were The One

You were the one I trusted
The one I enjoyed seeing
The one who put a smile on my face
The one who cared for me
The one I looked up to

You promised you would never leave
You disappeared
In a blink of an eye
Without warning
You just left

Never the same
Never will be
Knowing you are up there
Is OK
Hope you are safe.

Abigail Davis (13)
Gosford Hill School, Kidlington

Hi Grandad

Hi Grandad, up above
Do you remember me?
Do you remember how close we used to be?
I miss you a lot
You probably see me as a dot

Do you remember playing hide-and-seek?
I always used to peek
That was when I was four years old
Now I'm almost thirteen years old!

Caitlin Florence Ceri Laing (12)
Gosford Hill School, Kidlington

Internet

Oh Internet, fountain of knowledge
Helping me when I'm lost
Pulling me away from reality
You comfort me when I feel down
You are with me when I need you most
You can tell me anything that I need to know
You give me a guide to follow
Internet, I cherish you.

Evie Wiggins (13)
Gosford Hill School, Kidlington

Manchester

Terrorism
Bombs
Army and
War
Hoping for peace
Hoping for silence
Hundreds of violences
On the news
Shootings and killings
Innocent beings
Gone like a flash
Just want respect.

Jasmine Holmes (13)
Gosford Hill School, Kidlington

Hey Mister Bully!

Hey, Mister Bully
Heard you were there
Saw you make that guy fall to the ground again
I know what you say won't make your mother proud
But you carry on making that guy sad
It doesn't matter about his race
It doesn't matter about his weight
So why do you keep making him weak?

He's crying for help but you call him a snake
All you care about is what your gang thinks!
He tries hard in lessons, that's why you call him a geek

But why should he care what you think?
But he does because he is emotionally weak
Because of all the things you put him through this week

But hey Mister Bully, I hope you're proud - making that boy
feel like trash
He's a smart young boy, that's why you're bad
Jealous of the things you may never have

The thing that keeps him going is that his friends and family
are proud
You only bring your shame to the ones who care
Hey Mister Bully, what you got to say now?

Emma Fearn (14)
Kennet School, Thatcham

Shakespeare In School

'To be or not to be?' the teacher asks
I feel my existential crisis coming on fast
An intriguing question I must say
But I can't help but feel this is the wrong way
These characters should be acted, not at all read
For how can they act, when they're just in my head?

I'm not against reading, I really think it's swell
It can take you both to Heaven and Hell
But the reading of Shakespeare, especially in school
Makes it lacklustre and boring, causing students to drool
Shakespeare is amazing, according to me
So why must it suffer this cruel destiny?

Comedy, drama, violence and so much more
Teachers should make it less of a bore
We do an analysis explaining connotations
When there was no hidden meaning behind things like
ravens
Shakespeare wrote it to be enjoyed so much more
Now students do studies and it is more of a chore

I know it's sometimes hard for teachers to make things fun
But it cannot be a thing they should just shun
And I know playing movies all lesson is a bad move by the
teacher
But to the kids, they're more of a preacher

When teenagers find the words hard to comprehend
Hearing the tone of voice out loud is better than just asking
a friend

This poem may be even tedious to read
As the writer is the one that only plants the seed
To grow healthy, it must be fun and enjoyable
But if not, it will simply be trouble and toil
Shakespeare is an art that brings joy to so many
So don't let this generation miss out on any.

Natasha Low (13)
Kennet School, Thatcham

I've Seen It All

I've seen it. I've seen it with my own eyes
I've experienced it, I've felt the pain, the hurt, the anxiety of
it all
Makes you wonder... why you? Why now?
But in reality, it happens all the time

Bullying
It's everywhere, and impacts more than you know
Like when you're told you won't make it far in life
Because you're black
When a bully tells you to go back to your country
Because you're Asian
When they tell you you're dumb
Because you got a low test score
When they call you names
Just because they think it's fun

But the funny thing is, we were all born the same way
We are all human beings
We all have our own opinions
We were all given the freedom to live peacefully

How someone can segregate others
How someone can just pick on anyone at random and treat
them horribly
How someone thinks they have the audacity to bully
someone is beyond me
And believe me when I say that they have not got the right
or reason to bully you...

Always remember that whoever tries to bring you down is already beneath you
They don't need a real reason to bully you
They just do it
And know that you're not alone
As I've experienced the pain, the hurt, the anxiety of it all
And I've seen it. I've seen it all.

Yolanda Mkwezalamba (14)
Kennet School, Thatcham

Dictators Are Inhuman

Dictators have absolute power, freedom isn't to be seen.
In a democracy you believe it or not, in a dictatorship you
believe it or else...
Cruel leaders are replaced, only to have new leaders turn
cruel.
A lie told often enough becomes the truth, every human
right it abused.

Fatal leaders think death is the solution to all problems.
They don't want respect; they want people to fear them.
Who cares what their people say? Not the dictators, votes
are rigged!

Dictatorships are parodies of democracies,
You even have limited hair cut options!
Despotism is a long, awful crime; it shouldn't take place on
this planet.
The world should be united as a large democratic society,
Where people live in peace and have the human rights they
deserve.

Igor Kuroczycki (14)
Kennet School, Thatcham

Pets

Animals, some would say the best
Some would say the worst
Some even think of them as a curse

If you were looking after them
How would you treat them though?
Would you treat them well
Even in the snow?

You should care for them all of the time
After all they are living in your home
Make them happy, enjoy their life while they can
And never, ever leave them alone

So care for your animals, every day of your life
They don't like being lonely, especially in the dark
Make the most with them, enjoy it while it lasts
You never know it could be the last time they bark...

Sidney Whittle (14)
Kennet School, Thatcham

Poem About Video Games

Why I'm so passionate about playing video games
They're a time consumer
A joy maker
A geek gatherer
A money snatcher
A dream disrupter
A homework postponer
A bone wisher
A body craver
A story teller
A dexterity forger
A champion maker
A mind enhancer
An idea writer

I could go on and on
But I have demons to kill
A princess to rescue
And a world to save.

Max Benjamin Thomas (14)
Kennet School, Thatcham

Terrorism

Terrorism, what has the world come to!
Scared to go to London
Abundance of happiness taken away
With loved ones lost, blown up to decay

The universe must unite
In order to stop this horrific fight
Have peace and thankfulness for the blessings of life
Answers are definitely not found in a gun or a knife

Stop! Let's have a truce
Be friends again, no war on our hands.
USA and North Korea, the world as one
Working together with cohesive plans

Gangs! Stop the stabbing, Stop the shooting
What are you proving to yourselves?
Nights should be silent
Not a victim's picture, a photo on a shelf.

Rio Rae Farrell (12)
Millside School, Slough

What Makes Me Angry In My Life

What makes me angry in my life
Is when my friends have suffered strife

The stabbing of my friend O'Haye
Made me say things I shouldn't say
Hamza too was going to Dubai
And really was too young to die
Peer pressure caused him to jump that bridge
But his body must have hit a ridge
He couldn't swim that well anyway
Or that's what all my friends would say
Some say as a joke friends pushed him in
And that's why they said he couldn't swim
The bridge was high and the river deep
Just thinking about him, I can't sleep

He had beef with an ops in another town
It all started on Instagram
He invited this op to his home
Knowing he would not be alone
He didn't expect him really to come
When three of them turned up he felt quite dumb
Three turned up for a fist fight that day
He beat the hell out of them, so they ran away
They grabbed the machete out of the car
They didn't have to run very far

His name was Bigs because of his size
But all you could hear were his terrible cries
They stabbed him in the chest
But he still walked home
He died on the doorstep
In blood and alone.

Yahqub Mussa (15)
Millside School, Slough

Leave Us Alone

Leave us alone, we aren't rhinos without our horns.
Leave us alone, we have done nothing to you.
Leave us with our horns
Leave us with our dignity
Leave us at peace.
Leave us now.
Leave us alone, we're elephants that need our tusks.
Leave us, we haven't harmed you.
Leave us to survive.
Leave us to gather food.
Leave us at peace.
Leave us now.
Leave us alone, we're not snow leopards without our spots.
Leave us alone, we need our fur to survive in the weather.
Leaves with our bones intact.
Leave us with a life.
Leave us at peace.
Leave us now.
Leave us alone, we are tigers.
Leave us with our stripes and dignity.
Leave us with our lives.
Leave us to hunt.
Leave us at peace.
Leave us now or else
Leave us with our scales, we are the snakes.
Leave us with our fangs.

Leave us as snakes, not handbags.
Leave us to slither.
Leave us at peace
Leave us or you will get snuck up on
Leave us alone, we're the snakes of the river, we're crocodiles.
Leave us as crocodiles, not shoes.
Leave us with our snap.
Leave us to survive.
Leave us alone at peace
Leave us now or we shall snap at you.

Charlie Day (12)
Millside School, Slough

Upside Down

Upside down, upside down
I don't care if the school falls down
No more homework
No more maths
No more sitting in boring class

Teacher, teacher, I don't care
If I want I'm gonna swear
Is it black or is it white
I don't care, I'm gonna fight

Sports coach, sports coach
I don't care, you're just being unfair
Chase me round the garden path
I just want to have a laugh
Learners, learners everywhere
Don't pretend that you don't care
Try to work hard at school
Or else you'll end up becoming a fool

Stewart, Stewart that's not fair
Why is Manjit standing there?
He is black and you are white
I don't think you feel alright

It's obvious you don't care
Cos racism is so unfair
We don't accept that behaviour here
We don't want to live in fear.

Charlie Mcdonagh (12)
Millside School, Slough

A Poem About Bullying

Bullying is not cool
It just makes you look like a fool
Just follow the rules and stay in school
Teachers are no creatures
They will just help you
Not belt you
Bullies are not always in a crew
Sometimes they come in two
To abuse all of you
Who knew this would happen to you
Sometimes it's verbal
Sometimes it's physical
But it's not always visible
It is not fair
It is definitely not kind
Don't act like you are blind
To the effects of what you do next
No wonder why people get vexed
Go on Facebook, open your texts
Wonder if you are next.

Kiefer Betteridge (12)
Millside School, Slough

174

Daily Struggle

As the glistening sun simmers down from another day of
light.
The experiences that we have encountered throughout our
life continues to increase.
As humans we encounter an everyday challenge
For some it's a path of shining light but for others a gloomy
hole of darkness
We cannot choose the cards we have.

Cameron Balfour (11)

Millside School, Slough

The Beautiful Game

Each and every week it's that time again
Game time, thousands of individuals flock to the pearly
white gates of our stadium
It really is heaven, age, gender, race, occupation
None of it matters once inside
We all are one army working together in unison to uplift the
stadium
And to spur on our team, over land and sea

The atmosphere is magnifying and intense
The drums beat loud like thunder clouds overhead
We are all one
The adrenaline courses through our veins like a kid with
sugar sweets
We roar like proud lions protecting our own

The game is intense, fast paced, adrenaline fuelled
It's end to end, neck to neck
This is really magnificent
We are on our toes till the end
When we score we cheer louder than the roar of a thousand
soldiers.
This is truly a beautiful game.

Lennon Jay Wills (17)
Milton Keynes College, Leadenhall

Fire Emblem

This is a game I play every day
This is a game with a lot of memorable characters
This is a game with intertwining story plots
This is a game called Fire Emblem

There are sorcerers, Pegasus, knights, axe users
Healers and sword users
There are kings, queens, princes, princesses
Tacticians and knights
There are dragons, demons, Wyvern riders, bowmen and
animal shifters

This is a game I play every day
This is a game with a lot of memorable characters
This is a game that is an RPG
This is a game with intertwining story plots
This is a game called Fire Emblem and I will love it till the
end.

James Harvey (17)
Milton Keynes College, Leadenhall

Music...

Loud music blasting through your ears
Getting away from life for a moment
Time to think, relax and chill
Student life is hard, but music
Gets you away from all of that.

What is your passion for music?
Rock, pop, jazz, classical
There is so much to explore with music
Imagination running through your brain
Making you feel a mixture of emotions, feelings, opinions

Music makes the world go round
Music makes us happy or sad
Music is what makes my heart pump

What is your passion for music?

Chloe Jade Allen (18)
Milton Keynes College, Leadenhall

Where Is The Passion?

Society expects the best of us
Accept that we don't believe in high standards and
perfection
We believe in living our lives to our full extent

Society rumbles on about us
Having a bright and hopeful future
But yet alone they still frown upon the brave people
That try to take control of their life and be free

Hope is a word that is thrown around among society
Like a toy
But only the people that can catch the word hope and
persevere
Can defeat society.

Ben Casey (16)

Milton Keynes College, Leadenhall

The Family

We define ourselves by our family
A picture-perfect life yet
Society decides to tell the lie

We decide to share their names
Live in their place
Yet, inevitably, we end up alone

All alone in the world
Where no one can help you
You turn to your family
When you have no clue

They hold your secrets
Mother and Father unite
Knowing you're safe
When they tuck you in goodnight.

Leeanne Bairah (17)
Milton Keynes College, Leadenhall

Home

Home is the place where you rest your head
And home is the place where you stress less

Home is the place where your parents make dinner
And home is the place where you order takeout pizza

Home is the place where you sleep with a passion
And home is the place where you watch University
Challenge

Once you've gone there's chances to go back
But once home's gone there's no turning back.

Esme Clair Saunders (18)
Milton Keynes College, Leadenhall

The Same Old Stuff

What is there to be passionate about?
It's only a movie
Boring and dull
The same old stuff

When will it finish?
The constant pain
Rushing through my body

The same old stuff
Just end
Signing off
'The Breakfast Club'.

Joe Francis Farrell (17)
Milton Keynes College, Leadenhall

Her

I can't feel it
My heart has left home
I just want to abandon myself so I'll be alone
With the agony of thoughts building up inside of me
Where they're all caged up, please help me set them free

The rage inside brings me great pain
Sometimes, I do wonder if I'm still sane
I now sit alone and cry through the night
It's completely dark with no sign of a light

I blamed myself for the destruction you made
With no sign of joy my emotions start to fade
Trust; it's something great that we never shared
Only because you never bothered: you never cared

You told me stories of sympathy that I believed
My heart wasn't loved, cared for
It was thieved, brutally stolen, ripped right out of my chest
Just to be trampled on like all the rest

Now this is my goodbye letter
Hoping one day my life will get better.

Nicole Tessmer (15)
Sandy Upper School, Sandy

Different

I'm different
In fact, I'm so different that I'm weird
I'm so weird that I'm strange
And I'm so strange that I'm odd
And who wants to be friends with an odd person?
Being a teenager, one of my main ambitions was to be the coolest person ever
I wanted to be that girl with billions of Instagram followers
I wanted to be the girl who was envied rather than envy
So I started to change myself
I started to dress normally, I started to talk normally
I started to listen to the popular music
I started to hang around with the popular kids
I thought this would make me happy
But it didn't
I was sitting in with everyone
I was talking to everyone
However, I wasn't enjoying the conversations
I wasn't enjoying the people
Now I realise why, it was because I was ordinary
Me... me! I had lost myself!
So I started to change myself again
I started to lose all my friends, because they were never my friends

I only laughed at something if I thought it was funny
I started to style my hair how I liked it
I stopped wearing make-up so every time I look in the mirror
I see me

And now I'm lonely but I love it
I am true to myself, I accept everything and expect nothing
What people may think about me or say about me is none
of my business
I am true to myself
The people who are close to me are still a very big distance
away
Nobody in this world means more to me than my own
happiness
I may be strange
I may listen to dancehall music
When someone says dance I will happily whine my waist
And let people judge me
Because why should I allow someone to affect me and my
life

I look around me and see everyone stressed with their
problems
I look around and see people who claim they are friends
Yet are not friendly behind one another's back
And I find it funny, I find it funny and laugh because I
thought that's what I wanted
Yet here I am, I have found myself and I am true to myself

Embrace your weirdness and quirks because they are the things that make you unique
Trying to change yourself for other people isn't the right choice
Because on the way to discovering someone who is fiction you will lose yourself.

Lara Amy Richards (14)
Sandy Upper School, Sandy

Social World

Likes, likes, that's all that matters
Losing followers leaves kids in tatters
Constantly glued to their handheld device
Showing barely any signs of life

All around the world phones take over
Nowadays you get a signal on the cliffs of Dover!
More people talk on an interface
Than talking to each other face-to-face

Now we need to get things straight
Do we have to use them or can it wait?
Mothers call, 'Get off your phone!'
And all that comes back is, 'Leave me alone.'

And as new technology quickly descends
The social media feed never ends!
More apps and tech that makes our lives easier
But somehow they still make our lives busier!

Kids think that social media is a thriller
But deep down behind that screen, it's a killer.

Jamie McEvoy (15)
Sandy Upper School, Sandy

Why Is Our Society So Messed Up?

Society is fake, so negative, so stupid, so superficial, so
judgemental
Why is our society so messed up?
Self-worth measured by the number of followers and likes
As if society has been violently pierced with spikes
You have a circle of friends but just think...
How many of them will be there till the very end?
Through the rough times, tough times, harsh times
How many of each of your individual friends will stay for a
lifetime?
Just pause for a second, let me ask you a couple of
questions
How many times have you been called ugly, fat, worthless?
Is there a feeling inside telling you are too different
Beauty is now only in one certain category
A perfect face, a perfect body, a perfect weight
Why is society so ignorant?
How can there be an image, idea, interpretation
Of what a human should be?
We are all brought on this Earth to be different, not perfect
If you're skinny, you're anorexic
If you're thick, you're obese
If you're friendly, you're fake
See how society is... screwed

There are people suffering and people whispering behind
peoples' backs
Why is no one listening?
Promoting drugs and pity those in rehab
Promoting 'be yourself' and judge you for being you
Attacking teens, adults and children
Our society is an evil villain
I say this to anyone feeling pressurised to stay quiet
Staying still and following the path of hell
Feeling like they are weighed down by unrealistic
expectations
Society says you have to be and needs to call back to what
it means to be a human being
If society tells you, 'You are not beautiful, you are not worth
it.'
Stand up strong and say, 'Yes I am.'
Don't let society manipulate you and label you
Our society is so messed up.

Jakia Jasmin Nessa (15)
Sandy Upper School, Sandy

The Judge Of Society

Waiting for the judge to decide his life
Looking at his children and his wife
He tells them one last time
'You know it wasn't me.'

How many people die until we realise
Until we see the tears in their eyes?
Not just sticks and stones hurt
Words can break your bones too

It's done and they have his sentence
A lifetime for what?
And he's thinking to himself
What kind of world is this?

But it's not just hurt, lies and cries
There's good things too
Like school and friends
And time to socialise

He's leaving on his way to prison
He wrote a letter to his son
Saying maybe one day the world will change
But I'll see you one day.

Eleanor Rose Walker (13)
Sandy Upper School, Sandy

Omaha Beach D-Day

Hundreds of battleships flowed through the ocean
Soldier carriers full to the brim
With hopeless soldiers ready to fight
Or not
The weather, bipolar
Stormy, sunny, the weather throws the soldiers off guard
Soldiers are throwing up
Soldiers are afraid
Soldiers are regretting their decisions
It's too late
The soldiers are edging closer and closer
To their inevitable death
Suddenly, there's a halt
Commanders screaming, 'Go, go, go!'
The soldiers swarm out but it soon ends
Bullets flicker past the hopeless soldiers
Bullets kill the hopeless soldiers
All hope is low and lost
Only a few scared soldiers make it to cover
The rest lying dead
Dead on Omaha Beach.

Daniel Walker (15)
Sandy Upper School, Sandy

Unsocial Media

Every hour of every day I see a phone
People walking all alone
With headphones in and music playing
I start to wonder where they'll be staying from each house
Hotel
Or prison cell

I find it funny what people do for likes
Posting pictures or selfies with their new Nikes
These days it seems
All that matters is on a screen
But I don't care if you are at the gym
Or at home eating away your sin

I care more about seeing you face-to-face
Because we have forgotten what it means
To be a part of the human race
We don't need Instagram or Snapchat to talk
I would rather go out for a walk
A catch up
Before we get snatched up
By phones.

Caitlin Thomas (15)
Sandy Upper School, Sandy

Moment

When you turn your head
At just the right moment
And look out the window
And the clouds are pink
With a golden glow
And the sun slowly disappears

It never looked that way before
But it will only last a moment

So you stop for the moment
And breathe in the breeze
Focusing on the clouds
That now look like they're on fire
The golden outline the sun makes
The way they fade into the sky
Like pink smoke

If you turn back
The room looks darker than it was before
When you look again
The sky doesn't look the same
It's all changed
Now it's someone else's turn
To watch for the moment.

Ellie Brookes (15)
Sandy Upper School, Sandy

Why All This Hate?

Why all this hate?
Whether you choose to debate
Or ridicule someone's weight
You can't lie, it's growing at a fast rate
Are we too late?
Or maybe we just need to taste
Taste the fear people go through
Even if you don't know who
People are trapped in their house like some kinda zoo
What are we going to do?
Whether it was that boy you pushed or girl you hit
You have shredded them to bits
You think you're funny telling him he has nits?
We need to stand up for what's right
End every single fight
Don't be tight
Find the light
Rise to the height
As high as a kite
And do what's right.

Rio Joseph Samuels (15)
Sandy Upper School, Sandy

The Monster Behind The Screen

Social media can be a wonderful thing
It has turned into a worldwide thing
So many people can connect from afar
We can even find people that we didn't know in the past

But it can be a monster
It can take away your security and freedom
Pressure people not doing things to look good
We can hurt one another behind our screens
Without even knowing because we can't take our eyes off
the screen

What happened to the days where you could wear what you
want
Talk face-to face, go out
Without boys and girls talking about how you look
Who you're with and without the whole world knowing what
you are doing.

Shannon Page Lewinton (15)
Sandy Upper School, Sandy

Life

One hundred years down the road
How will you be remembered?
A lonely life, inside you're starved
Or making the most of it, which was intended?
A caring, compassionate soul
Or one filled with hatred and spite?
When you've grown up and become old
Thinking about your life in the middle of the night
What will you recall?
Good times, bad times, mistakes, regrets
How many times you got up, how many times you fell
In the fate of any threats
How did you face it?
Standing up, bold and tall
Or did you give up and quit?
This is your life, you must've used it all
Once it's gone, it's gone forever.

Jordan James Irvin (15)
Sandy Upper School, Sandy

Love

Today I witnessed love
I once thought I'd never feel love
Never see love
Never hear love
I thought it was just a word
Just four letters thrown together
But I opened my mind today and
Saw what was before me
Love was all around or was it not
Is love nature, is love pure
I'm not sure
Is love the thing you feel when you wake up every day?
Is love the bright light shining in the sky every morning?
Is love what I'm missing in my life?
Do you know what love is?
Does anyone know?
I need to know, I see the sky turning blue
And yet I never get close to the answer
Did I discover love?

Caitlin Pearce (14)
Sandy Upper School, Sandy

Dancing Feet

Dancing, prancing, living the dream
My feet don't stop moving
I feel like I am in glee
I dance night and day
With no worry to the world
I know I'm great
I don't need to be told

'Ella,' I hear shouting from below
'Stop moving your feet.'
OMG, I'm about to blow
My feet hurt with pain
I push harder every night
I won't let my dream disappear from my sight

My shoes are hung
And I am finally done
My feet won't stop dancing
Because I'm
Dancing, prancing, living the dream.

Ella Symonds (14)
Sandy Upper School, Sandy

Untitled

I miss you and love you
And you know that I do
And although I try
I can't find a reason why
I can't drown my demons
They know how to swim
But I know somehow I will find a way to win
Like you taught me to do
I love and miss you
I will always keep you in my heart
Although it feels like a poisonous dart
It keeps hitting me through and through
Just know that I don't blame you
With every fibre of my being
I know that soon we will be meeting
Maybe some time when I am sleeping
But I will never stop believing.

Demi Hopkins (15)
Sandy Upper School, Sandy

Alone

Shattered to the bone
That girl was left alone
She looked dead but still alive
Her face was crinkled
But not to be wrinkled
But why was she left alone?

In the darkness she stared
But yet nothing was there
Then she realised she wasn't alone
An odd-looking figure
Reflected back from the mirror
But was it really there?

She started to mumble
Turned around with a stumble
She wanted to scream
But no words could be found
She closed her eyes
And fell to the ground.

Jessica Woodward (14)
Sandy Upper School, Sandy

Game Of Life

They tell me it's just a game
But here is where I'll make me a name
Gain the fame
In this game

Some might call me lame
For living in a game
But isn't life just the same
Only there's no save points or quick loading
Oh and the story is just so boring

But I guess it's not so bad
Sometimes it's good, sometimes it's bad
A range of emotion
It can cause quite the commotion

So life is just a bad game
Still I guess it's not that lame.

Kye McCann (15)
Sandy Upper School, Sandy

Chocolate

My favourite food is chocolate
It's in cakes, biscuits and other things
Chocolate is a food that brings people together
It's like like a feather
But doesn't last forever
I bet you have already had some today
When people see it they say hooray
It's all of our guilty pleasures
We try to make it our only treasure
But sadly it always disappears
It's one of my greatest fears.

Emily Alice Garlick (15)
Sandy Upper School, Sandy

Next Time

Next time you leave your lights on
Think about where the ice is from
Next time you have a big fire
Remember the polar bears are tired

Next time you leave the heating on
That's what the polar bears are grieving
You wonder why the ice is getting warm
Maybe because all the plug sockets are on

Next time just think...

Daniel Truett (14)
Sandy Upper School, Sandy

Bouncy Balls

Balls are big, balls are small
Balls are round and some are tall
Balls are bouncy when they reach the sky
Some are squishy, some are slimy
Some are tiny and some are shiny
Tick, tick, tock
When the hand has reached the top
I come out and play
Every single day to play
Love balls so much
I just want to say hush, hush, hush.

Maddy Jakes (14), Daniel & Rosie
Sandy Upper School, Sandy

Lucky Day

I was roaming through the streets of Dover
Only to find a four-leaf clover
I turned bright and I was in delight
But then I found a range rover
I thought it wasn't mine
But then only to see my name written all over
I said to myself, 'It's been a very lucky day.'

Riley Jay Lewis Evans (14)
Sandy Upper School, Sandy

A Beautiful Place

The environment is a beautiful place
With trees, birds and lots of space
And the grass stands tall and proud
But we take advantage of the living
And all it does is keeps on giving
Oxygen, materials and lots of space
But after all the environment is a beautiful place.

Nathan Thomas Costin (15)
Sandy Upper School, Sandy

People

Lots of different people
Lots of different classes
Lots of different people
And some that wear glasses

There are short people
Tall people
And some just in-between
But they're all the nicest people
That I have ever seen.

Emily Kirton (13), Chloe & Lola
Sandy Upper School, Sandy

I Love You

I love you
I love you a lot
Even more than Jelly Tots
You make me smile
And it goes on for a while
You're really funny
And cute like a bunny
I'd sneak out the house
As quite as a mouse.

Shardaya Callari (14)
Sandy Upper School, Sandy

The Turtle

Do people really not care
About the sea, and all that's there
For this is my home after all
It's basically my big swimming pool
For all of those who put stuff in my home, like litter
Why? You're just all sour and bitter
Before you throw stuff in the sea
Please think of me
This is where I live, under this rock
Birds fly over in great big flocks
Fish swim from coral to coral
Down here it's very floral
Oh do people really not care
About the sea and all that's there?
For this is my home after all
It's basically my big swimming pool
So before you throw stuff in the sea
Oh please think of me.

Ellena Rose Sandford (12)
The Milton Keynes Academy, Leadenhall

My Mask

Today my mask isn't made of plastic
It's made of paranoia
An emotion that's slowly tearing me away inside
My mask feels too weak
As if at any moment
At any time
It would fall off

I'm the ugly duckling
In a pond of ducks
But I'm a swan
But they can't see that
So they stare and they judge
Right from my bill
Down to my feet
So I carry on
As a duck

When will the time come
Where I will no longer need my mask
When can I feel free
From this burden of everyone's judgements?
But the world cannot stop judging
It's what they do best

What happens one day
If the wind blows too powerfully?

And gradually, bit by bit
Tears my mask right off my face?

The world stares
All piercing eyes on me
Watching
Judging
But do they see me
Or do they see *me*?

Husnah Iqbal (12)
The Milton Keynes Academy, Leadenhall

Family

Families are people
Who care about you
My family is special
Your family are too

Mothers and fathers
Brothers and sisters
Grandmas and grandpas
And so many others

One family is big
While another is small
Some families have children
And some, none at all

When we're together
Or far, far apart
The people I love
Fill the map of my heart.

Ittay Socosote (12)
The Milton Keynes Academy, Leadenhall

Tyson

Tyson, I love you
You were my friend
We had fun times together
The days we said we were going to the beach
When actually it was the vets
Tyson, I love you
You were my friend
Tyson, I love you
Always fly high
Your eyes are like shimmering stars in the moonlit night.

Sascha Lilianah Hall (12)
The Milton Keynes Academy, Leadenhall

Aiming Higher

Sometimes all you need is a push, a kick,
To get you back on track,
To get you onto your feet, we all go through rough times
Wanting to move on, let go of things
But really all you need to do is spread your wings

Dreaming and wishing won't get you to your destination
But working hard will, not giving up, as well as dedication
So just stop wishing, complaining and start doing
Only this way you will find yourself succeeding, improving

Not everything comes easy, not all decisions are right
But you should learn from your mistakes
And not give up without a fight
Out there you can always find new opportunities
It could be your chance to shine or time to make great
memories

You told me to sit back, so I'm going to work harder
You told me to sit back, so I'm going to work harder
You told me to give up, so I'm going to aim higher
You called me weak, well you were wrong
Thinking I gave up on this, yet I'm writing this song

You think this is all stupid, you play your annoying games
But you see I don't get things handed on a plate
I work hard for it

I try my best, I dedicate myself to this
Because of the feeling in my chest

There are no tricks to success, no easy way out, no elevator
goes that high
So you'll have to take the stairs and climb
Fear will always come but you shouldn't be scared to try
Remember that your future is in your hand
So if you aim for the moon, the moon is where you'll land

Not everything comes easy, not all decisions are right, but
you should learn from your mistakes
And not give up without a fight
Out there you can always find new opportunities
It could be your chance to shine or time to make great
memories

You told me to sit back, so I'm going to work harder
You told me to sit back, so I'm going to work harder
You told me to give up, so I'm going to aim higher
You called me weak, well you were wrong
Thinking I gave up on this, yet I'm writing this song

People will say things, to put you off, but instead of
believing it
Make it disappear, like dust with a cloth
Don't be scared to try again, or lose a fight
Because maybe next time you can make it right

Pick yourself up, don't lose the fight before the start
Pick yourself up, don't let anyone break your heart
Pick yourself up, do it today, don't get discouraged by what others say

Not everything comes easy, not all decisions are right
But you should learn from your mistakes, and not give up without a fight
Out there you can always find new opportunities, it could be your chance to shine
Or time to make great memories

You told me to sit back, so I'm going to work harder
You told me to sit back, so I'm going to work harder
You told me to give up, so I'm going to aim higher
You called me weak, well you were wrong
Thinking I gave up on this, yet I'm writing this song.

Julia Galbierczyk (15)
The Westgate School, Slough

Untitled.43

I feel at ease when I get major waved
'Cause nowadays everybody's taking aim
Back-stabbers stained my trust like ugly stains of Gatorade
Whispers scratch my ego like a jagged rusty razor blade

And still everybody says I've changed
It's called growin' but the more I notice everybody stays the same
I got some accusations and I don't know who's gon' take da blame
Cuz struggling for a basic wage is the only way to make some change

Well where I'm from that ain't true
We've got door-to-door salesmen dressed up in tracksuits
Bags on their hip makin' sales like retail
Keep all their product in their bags like a shallow female

Life's a Rubix Cube competition but with colour-blind contestants
Everyone so focused on the outcome, they ain't thought about the entrance
Stepping over people below 'em 'cause they don't see helping 'em can help you grow too
If you don't control your own hunger
There's a day when it will own you.

Owais Ahmad (17)
The Westgate School, Slough

Untitled

You get told hate is a strong word
From all the rumours you heard
People trying to get you down
Trying to carve a permanent frown
Why does the world make sure that's how you feel
People forget that as humans we are not made of steel
You thought love is number one priority
But people being nosy, driven by curiosity
Hate spreads like fire
In your mind they are a liar

Wake up hoping for a better day
Hop out of bed, drop to your knees before you pray
Hope is always lost
It comes at a cost
You ride the brutal roller-coaster ride
To feel the mighty pride
Search day and night for your spark and liberate your light
Once you find it you will shine bright
You dash the negative vibes away
Sail on to have a marvellous end of day

You walk alone this empty road
To get your mind away from the heavy load
Remember greatness is not found in success
It is found in all your hard-working stress

The underestimated potential that is hidden in your smile
Will dial your future trial
Your capability is more than just a grade
Because we all know you will cut through like a blade
All you have to do is put your own twists to the magic
And make sure you don't panic

Always remember life is a gift
So don't feel like the foggy mist
Having a great big laugh is what we are here for
So pick yourself up from the floor
And be inspired
To get admired
Appreciate the moments that come by
Because they make the real night sky
The gazing stars make a smile
To get you far that extra mile

Your heart beats and beats
To make empty roads feel like home streets
You have to keep life real
With each and every meal
But really is that the case?
I don't think in this place
Live life to the fullest
You may get hit by a bullet
Now that's part of life
So there is no need to strife

At the end of the day
No clouds are grey
That clearly means be yourself
No need to be the elf
Your struggles
Never show your stumbles
The mistakes you commit
Show you are committed
Your future dream
Should now be your number one stream.

Breerah Mahmood (15)
The Westgate School, Slough

A Pen In A Pencil Case

I have lots of chew marks
And the others don't have any
They have seen lots of people
And I haven't seen many
I'm old
My colours aren't bold
I don't have much ink left in me
But I guess that's what comes when you're a pen in pencil case
As the zip zooms across above me
I see a light that is warm and lovely
The giant hand that comes in
Takes the highlighter to the bin
I get pushed to the bottom
And darkness is all I see
I'm alone, I'm afraid and no one is with me
I dread the day when they take me out
And look at me and loudly shout
It's broken! And they throw me away
Oh how I dread that day
But, I'm only a pen in a pencil case.

Tegan Condra (12)
The Westgate School, Slough

Growing Up

The butterfly hatched from the cocoon and that's when you
realise nothing stays the same
No one around you is to blame
And your closest friend, you can't remember her name
You hate the way you look, because we are taught to judge
by the cover of the book
Because if it's not eye-catching, it's time-snatching

Welcome to growing up
Where you spend most of your teenage years throwing up
'Eating disorder' is your main label
You dread sitting at the table
Saying you're just sleepy
And it hurts you deeply

Welcome to growing up
You'll starve yourself every day
And for this your body will pay
You want to fit in
And its killin' - you
You wanna know how it feels to be perfect
You wanna feel worth it

Welcome to growing up
You lost your closest friend
And you feel like your life's come to an end

You feel hollow inside
'I'm so broken,' you cried
Now your tears have dried
You try moving on
But everything goes wrong

We are told to love the body we are taught to hate by our peers
Constantly introduced to new fears
Same ours and theirs
Never thinking about the words we speak yet continuously stressing over the calories of everything we eat

Welcome to growing up.

Aisha Nadeem (16)
The Westgate School, Slough

The Art Of Breaking

There is an art in the ways of breaking someone
To first mould them into a perfect toy to play with
Make them love you, crave you, want you
Because your facade has been perfected for this certain task
Then destroying them from the inside first
Rip out their heart, destroy their hope, make them vulnerable
So beautiful watching their emotions overwhelm them
To the point of physical pain
Pain to which they raise a shaking hand to their chest and feel their heart break, little by little
And you know you've won but it's so... unsatisfactory
Because they can still be mended with tender care
For one can't truly be broken 'til there is no way to fix it
So you continue, smashing, tearing and hurting
Make them feel hated because they are
Because you ruined them
Made people turn their backs to that innocent hurt soul
Made them feel so alone
Till you're left with a phantom of the person you knew
A small ghost to haunt you, something to keep as a reminder
On the high shelf of your room
To be in its place with the others

Not something you broadcast to the world
But something you go back to for inspiration for something
new
And there will always be something new
And things to break.

Isha Maqsud (14)
The Westgate School, Slough

Syria

Have you seen it?
It's terrible isn't it?
Every time I see those little kids' faces on the TV
It strikes my heart like someone has just stabbed me
I really don't know what has happened to humanity
It's like everyone is our enemy
Don't have a place to call home
No one to call mom, dad, daughter, son or even friend
It hurts
It hurts to know that there is a little baby buried underneath
a ground... alive
Maybe it's faith
But it's wrong, very wrong
Us...
We...
Stand here thinking about what we are going to do next
Or where we are gonna go next
But what we don't understand is what the future holds
It all depends on what we are doing now!
Now is your starting point
Now is the time for you to work hard
Because hard work darling, always pays off
It's now or never

So here I stand with my little voice
Asking you to make a difference
Asking you to make a change
Asking you to save the country of thousands...
Syria.

Zaafira Azhar (14)
The Westgate School, Slough

A Statement

What god expects love to be hate
For the dire, immasculine or effeminate
For the burning
Secret
Passion
Of love
Who deems it so love is godly...

Unless you love that man?

What god decrees that he loves you all
Unconditionally
Unless, of course, you challenge his conditions

What god sits in his ivory tower
Imprinting his gaze
Printing off his perfect acolytes
Who tell you that your love is not love because some bloke
wrote it so,
Through eight different languages, 2,000 years ago?

And I know, I know
That whist we gaze
Into the same, empty, crystalline night
Miles, hundreds apart
I know that you feel it... me, feel me
And I know that I love you

Regardless
Of who you love, or where you love them
In a way no god can,

Because that is love
And what you were taught
Well, that's hate.

Oliver Fiore (16)
The Westgate School, Slough

Autumn

You hear the little pitter-patter drops of rain
The luminous rays of the bright, golden sun
To go and run about and spend time as a family
To enjoy the moment
The days where you can cuddle up indoors when it's winter
But can anybody describe when the leaves fall freely
And you collect them to jump in or use for a piece of art
I know what it's called, it's called autumn
You remember the memories of the red and burnt orange leaves
Hitting the ground
The children's smiles when they come out
But we all grow up
But I will remember those days
My memories
And I plan to remember them, and never forget.

Cassady Byrne (12)
The Westgate School, Slough

YOUNG WRITERS INFORMATION

We hope you have enjoyed reading this book – and that you will continue to in the coming years.

If you're a young adult who enjoys reading and creative writing, or the parent of an enthusiastic poet or story writer, do visit our website **www.youngwriters.co.uk.** Here you will find free competitions, workshops and games, as well as recommended reads, a poetry glossary and our blog.

If you would like to order further copies of this book, or any of our other titles, then please give us a call or visit **www.youngwriters.co.uk.**

Young Writers
Remus House
Coltsfoot Drive
Peterborough
PE2 9BF
(01733) 890066
info@youngwriters.co.uk